HEART-SPARKING
PERFORMANCE

IT'S ABOUT CONSCIOUSNESS
(AND IT'S ABOUT TIME)

JON ROOT

ARS METAPHYSICA

an imprint of Sunbury Press, Inc.
Mechanicsburg, PA USA

an imprint of Sunbury Press, Inc.
Mechanicsburg, PA USA

For information about special discounts for bulk purchases, please contact Sunbury Press Orders Dept. at (855) 338-8359 or orders@sunburypress.com.

To request one of our authors for speaking engagements or book signings, please contact Sunbury Press Publicity Dept. at publicity@sunburypress.com.

ISBN: 978-1-62006-322-4 (Trade Paperback)

Library of Congress Control Number: Application in Process

FIRST ARS METAPHYSICA EDITION: 2019948918

Product of the United States of America
0 1 1 2 3 5 8 13 21 34 55

Set in Bookman Old Style
Designed by Crystal Devine
Cover by Terry Kennedy
Edited by Lawrence Knorr

Continue the Enlightenment!

CONTENTS

THE 'WHAT'

There was a specific intention when I released my first novel, *Life, The Spiritual Sport*. Sharing a tough story wasn't the primary driver. What started as an 'open letter' to my daughter, sharing parts and pieces of challenges I had endured while she and I were apart, finished with an unintended consequence. Replaying life's highs and lows, how I was able to rise above or cope with challenges mirrored many lessons, teachings and experiences gleaned from decades of successes and challenges. Bubbling up behind the silent communication to my daughter was a very sharp point.

The one point that distilled from all other points of reference was a discernible heart-sparked vision wanting to frame up performance and transformation in a new way. Unique teachings from unique lessons learned and applied across different expressions. All things sport, training and competition, I started at age seven with no dream of grandeur. Twenty-seven years hence, I finished my career as an Olympic gold medalist and world champion, blessed to have compiled records and successes with eleven other men who I respected and admired.

In parallel was a personal (spiritual) journey to unwind and unravel the ball of angst and aggression that had condensed my psyche growing up in a very dysfunctional home environment. These undercurrents were contained in the vent of sports and competition, but with retirement, discord eventually surfaced, reflecting a need to alter and modify early coding. Dense and intense just a part of what and who I had become. The intensity eventually imploded, over and over again.

As a young adult athlete, it became apparent, I was born with good wiring. A naïve buck rumbling in, trying to get proficient at any team sporting activity I could attend riding my bike. There wasn't an idol or an inspiration I dreamed of emulating, I just enjoyed engaging, learning, trying to be part of a team pack.

It started out without fanfare in my backyard, playing by myself, imaginary shot clock buzzer-beaters, slap shots from thirty feet into narrow creases, fullback runs with five defenders on my back desperately trying to bring me down as I crossed the goal line to win in overtime, crashing on the edge of my grass yard, hands up triumphantly, mocking those vanquished.

Rarely were there the cocky 'ballers' back in the day. Mostly sweaty, shirtless men bouncing off each other were just barking and blathering. There were always a few however that played with a noticeable disposition. They were quiet but quietly dominant. You played. All out, all the time. Things happened, or they didn't. You won, or you lost. Sports kept my body, brain, and spirit consumed with a never-ending series of problem-solves. My brain liked it and my physical body responded in kind.

The early years started with tee-ball morphing into baseball, basketball, and flag football. If I got bored, I signed up for ceramics, art classes and the impromptu double dutch jump rope challenges in the park. Hard for me to say why I never dreamed of becoming a professional athlete, let alone an Olympic champion. By the time I finished 8th grade, even thinking about going to college was a distant vision. The tangible things brought me comfort and security, understanding my arm strength, speed, movement, throwing mechanics, seeing situations develop before they actually did. The only reason I started playing volleyball was I broke my throwing arm after a nasty hip check playing basketball.

The lesson from an upperclassman a bitter one. The compound fracture in my arm provided plenty of time to simmer. The simmering soon caused one door to close, and another to open. Sitting on the sidelines in a full arm cast, watching potential teammates toss back and forth in spring baseball was a gut wrench. Turned out that viewing session was an opportunity the volleyball coach had been waiting for. A whip for a right arm, good hand-eye coordination, fast-twitch movement translated perfectly into the sport of volleyball. He enticed me to come to play summer league once my arm was healed. I never went back to play another sport.

There were multiple tipping points along the path, however, in hindsight, since the age of seven sports was an upward trajectory without a major fail. Twenty years of whole mind, body development, opportunity, hard work, timing, and a little good luck produced key performances at the right time. Blend good reflexes, speed, coordination, a proclivity to heal quickly, and just the right amount of angst and anger, I was a good sport chemistry experiment waiting to happen.

What was never spoken about in my childhood added an asterisk to this journey. I was one of those kids who grew up in a broken household. Broken in more ways than I could understand at seven. An unfortunate series of events between Mother and me forced an early decision to ascertain what was for my best and highest good. I couldn't deal with unpredictability, confusion, and chaos. All those elements combined and eventually frothed me into a hard choice. The choice was to leave home before my twelfth birthday. Oddly, it never really registered as that big of a deal. Something needed to change.

A tough run it was around my house from ages seven to eleven. Confused, always on eggshells wondering what was coming next, there was a cloudy perspective on what normal was supposed to be. I tried not to blame, go all ballistic because someone was acting crazy. You want to believe, operate as you do believe everything will one day just be better, different. It's impossible to understand the density of challenges mom and dad dealt with as individuals and parents. But like it or not, we are subject to their unconscious patterns and behaviors.

One day out of the emergency room, a fresh white plaster cast around a double leg fracture incurred while on a solo Christmas Eve bike outing in Carmel, California, life quickly took a different path. Miserable, throbbing from the pain, I found myself on the receiving end of an emotional and physical outburst which forever changed my course. It started as bickering and arguing between

Mother and Grandmother. It ended up a fight between me and Mom, except I couldn't move.

The doctor said it would take the better part of five months before I was back to sports. I grimaced and squirmed knowing something needed change. Going through the gyrations, pretending things were copasetic was no longer an option. Thus, a personal pledge was made. Once I could run, I was done. I would figure it out on the fly. The decision didn't weigh me down, it felt freeing. The fear of what was coming next vanished as fast as I did.

So, I waited it out, let the healing do its thing. Six weeks before my twelfth birthday freedom was visible, white plaster dust from a handheld circular saw billowed up and out into the examining room. In grand metaphor, a leg was hatched from its casing, freshly healed and ready to a part of the team again. Mom got the story I was going to stay with a friend for a few days. A few days turned into many weeks. My second family knew what was up, but they gave me love, acceptance, and space to relax.

As one might imagine, this kind of path comes with extra baggage. I was insightful enough at a later point in my upbringing to admit this box of junk would have to be revisited. I had no idea when that time would present itself, but I just knew. I boxed it all up and shoved that imaginary chest of gagged gremlins deep on a high shelf. Little could I have realized, 'later' would consume the better part of twenty more years.

Close friends have heard me quip that I credit sports for saving my life. It wasn't the showcase of playing sports, rather the ability to vent off the emotional residue of fear and insecurity. Essentially, sports saved me from me. There was so much coal in my caverns, fueling my fire was a non-issue. It was retiring from full-time training and competing which created a monstrous grey zone where identity and clarity were cloudy. Without the burn-in high exertion, I was lost. There was in fact, too much free time spent mulling, wondering, and pondering.

The mere thought of foraging through my emotional clutter, doing some rearranging in my psyche was dreadful. But deep down I knew the work was inevitable. This acknowledgment started a very long unwinding process which brought with it, deep dives into personal growth, sacred teachings, mystical traditions, and years of participation in purification rituals across different spiritual platforms, Buddhist, Hindu, Christian, and Native American. Sacred ceremonies (non-psychedelic) consisting of the intentional sacrifice of food and water for days on end. Side by side the experiences gleaned from high-intensity physical training, a paradigm changer.

These events of sacred separation were diametrically opposed experiences to belief structures instilled at an early age. It was let go versus hold on tight. There was zero emphases placed on the interchange of the physical body and metaphysical systems, how they could be identified, managed (or leveraged) and applied to all performance and phases of change. How and why on God's green earth could physical performance, competition, besting others, becoming a champion, be influenced by such mumbo jumbo as energetic balance, self-discipline, positivity, intuition, that elusive 'sixth' sense. *Hogwash, boy. You need to toughen up, wash your mouth out with soap, then clean out that mess of ideas stuck between your ears.*

Thus, I kept two very clean, well-organized compartments neat and separate. Sports, all things physical, everything learned about metrics, force and mind/body development as it related to 'progress, had its own playground. You think this and then you do that. No back-talk boy. Yes, sir. I didn't push back, ask questions, or wonder if there was an alternate reality. Progress was only possible through repetition and practice.

The other compartment in my imaginary playground stored my secret box. Hidden from plain sight, this box contained all the dark stuff in my life outside of sport, resentment, anger, confusion, hurt. So, I stuffed it somewhere I pretended it couldn't hurt. This was the place to dwell and have real conversations with imaginary people I couldn't see but believed existed. It didn't feel safe to share with real people, so I never did.

If there was no place for back-talk in sports, what would come about if I mentioned the imaginary people actually talked back, and with very sound advice no less. This was my definition of spiritual, and it was better kept quiet. My sacred separation, the imagery, the longing, the hero's journey, the contemplation. What they referred to as the metaphysical stuff had no place in where

I was going with my athletics. You want to be the boot or the ass that gets kicked by that boot? Yeah, yeah, I get it.

Beyond high school athletics, the next wave of concepts and conversations bridging physical and metaphysical truths and tenets were discovered. How to consciously affect performance, including the ability to grow, evolve past limitations, challenges, conflicts or life trials. Coming into Stanford as a top recruit cultivated a personal attitude of wanting Stanford to get as much as they could from their investment in me. Falling short on that personal promise was not in the choice matrix. Failure was not an option.

In my days at Stanford, it was difficult to find sports psychology or practitioners embracing the Eastern concepts of mind, body, and spirit. I read up on what I could find during free time in the library stacks covering sport development and mental training. Yet, without an experienced mentor around to guide and instruct, the concepts remained just that. Imagery, visualization, imagination in constructing the desired vision, mentally mapping out a peak performance was the plan. The power in that plan would eventually reveal the 'magic in our minds.'

From a concept to experiencing that concept in application we find conviction, the truth embedded in all aspects of our experience. After years against world-class competition, those times playing in the 'zone,' you embrace there is something bigger than our individual variables in action. You come to understand that mental toughness can be cultivated. That paying attention to energies beyond our touch can be tapped and channeled for our benefit. Divine aid in those years was summed up in the expression *Be the Ball*.

The physical and the metaphysical seeds are what they are when kept to their own Petri dishes. It took many years to fully understand there is magic to be had when we engage separate operating systems to mix, play and support the other. As a natural tinkerer, it is akin to overturning a full toolbox onto the center of the floor, identifying known tools, clearing out the lonely, unpaired, bent and trodden items, then exploring with curiosity how some tools can serve different needs and situations. You want to figure out how something works, take it apart. Reverse engineering of sorts.

When both boxes of stuff, the objective mind/body tools, and the more interpretive emotional/energetic items are tossed onto the floor, mixed together, then separated again, we appreciate with a higher degree of awareness, how these pieces, tenets of truth, mix and match to produce amazing things. That the whole is greater than its parts.

"Mind, body, and spirit" is convenient as an expression of unity, but there is more to it. There are the individual operating systems we all deal with, then there is the integration of these processes which we all can leverage, ultimately producing greater impact towards things we wish to co-create.

Coming full circle from my opening tag, the 'what' is a clarified intention to help others from what I have learned and applied. Higher highs and lower lows reflected a range of successes mirrored by great challenges. At some point, my relationship with life needed structural change. Everything felt like a competition devoid of any divine mojo and it felt like I was losing more than winning. It was straightforward to pinpoint the mental purpose, but not the spiritual purpose in my commitment. I didn't always make the 'right' choice at times, but I improved by striking out less.

The What as an intention covers over thirty years of deep dives, pulling out the pearls, stringing them a different way and with different materials. Instead of just talking about consciousness, let's see where we can string disparate materials together. Spice things up a bit. Better yet, let's connect the dots and see what is body-mapped. The 'Whatmap,' with appropriate metaphors, becomes a reference manual for performance and change.

It's not easy work, but the fine-tuning is worth the work. Competition, challenge, conflict or commitment, ongoing reasons to continually raise your game. Either a higher spot on the mountain requiring something better, more efficient, or from a place proverbially face down muttering, 'I can't take this anymore,' there is always a way up and a way out. Always is and always will be. It's about consciousness, and it's about time.

THE 'WHY'

Empty **and alone** next to a coveted bottle of Meritage stood one long-stem wine glass. The landscape elicited an audible sigh. Not how I envisioned. It wasn't a sigh generated from one dominant emotion. Like the wine, the depressive moan was a blended varietal, resentment dominant, supported by spices of anger. The finish was equally strong, bold, distinctive. Fine flavors evaporating into another expectation that the next sip would be lighter, finer. A voice from somewhere inside my head brought a pang of responsibility. *Slow your roll and get a grip.*

Red, my rescue dog, sat patiently on his hinds as I leaned into a high tilt, forearms resting on the granite bar top. His tongue was hanging far out the side of his mouth bouncing from the panting. He looked happy. He didn't understand and that was a good thing.

An extended stretch of life struggles found me tired before I even dropped into the lean towards a glass half full. Hoping wasn't lining up with reality. What I thought was over, apparently was nowhere close to over. *Law of substitution, law of substitution,* anxiously muttered over and over, *don't drop into victim mode.* Slowing the rhythm of my breath converted a pending panic attack to just superficially pondering the dreaded 'why.' The universe seemed to have a follow-up lesson in store.

The early portion of that year ushered in a few fleeting months where it felt as though the tough stuff was finally in my rearview mirror. The joy of Easter lingered over our seventeen elite regional club volleyball championships. The girls really got after it, clinching a coveted berth to the Junior National Championships. The mental replay of girls rushing the court, hugging, happy, humbled, brought a smile of pride.

I readied for a second sip of wine. Halfway in the up action, another thought. We had a shot to finish top ten in the country. Yes, we do, I said out loud to no one in particular with another smile. Pride. It has its moments. For the first time in months, my mental chatter was not composed of worry, anxiety or angst about whatever was next. The relief was short-lived.

Two days later, nervously fiddling in the anteroom of my surgeon's office, clumsily thrashing through magazines to keep, hands, eyes, and mind busy, all I could muse was *what are the odds?*

In between page flips, my brain was running a productive calculation exercise. My guess of twenty percent didn't end up winning the drawing. Dr. Bruno's third sentence into our greeting initiated a momentary glaze out. *Pardon me, Doc. Can you say that again? Not quite sure I understood what you just said.*

His assistant stood taller, rigid, deadpanned, staring right through me. You have cancer. Prostate. Early detection. You're 'lucky' he said. In limbo, the slow curve caught me frozen for a called strike three. "When do you think you can schedule surgery?" Numb and dumb would be appropriate enough as a descriptive.

Five days later, a follow-up quake. My stepmother Ruthann (the better half of my mothering tandem) died from stroke complications. It was hard to parcel the sadness between my own grieving, and that of my Father's. Half expecting empathy for my condition required flipping an internal script hastily prepared. Forty-six years of marriage is a long bond and truth be told, there was more concern he might want to prematurely be on his own way. My lips started to part, full intention looking for the crack in the conversation to share my news. What was supposed to come out of my mouth instead drizzled silently down each cheek.

Hours and hours of porch pondering, half-baked, were spent trying to get my head around equally fortified doses of sadness and fear. Whispers of what the fuck gassed out, head tilted back, gazing up to the heavens, palms simultaneously slapping down on the worn wooden deck. There was no physical feeling. So empty was the 'something,' I couldn't feel a thing.

Hours every day not moving, sitting quietly on the deck, I grieved. Red dog hovered afoot and never left my side. Chunks of the day consumed convincing myself to just ride out the set. *Stay on your board, just float, don't make any drastic choices.* The lone, daily dose of inspiration, a copy of my own performance map taped above the light switch in my bedroom. I was tempted to give it the finger with a verbal follow, but logic prevailed.

Mockingly, rubbing the 8" by 11" graphic, desperately calling the genie to come out just one more time. C'mon dude, I really need you right now. At that moment, in mental quicksand, another comeback seemed conceptually elusive. Speaking to me, myself and I, a moment of weakness. I knew I wasn't going to give up, but I found myself asking 'why me.' Thank goodness there were no witnesses to my submission. My chin dropped towards my chest in firm resolution. *I can't do this anymore God. I need some help.*

Shut off and getting more cynical with each passing week created a mass of negative energy. For a Myers-Briggs intuitive thinker, not a fundamentally sound mode of being. A plan was one thing. This was not something when thinking it through was going to solve much. The immediate search and recovery effort focused solely on retrieving one scrap of positivity.

The life bond with my stepmother was coursing its way through my being. She had become a very stabilizing, grounding influence. A surprise given I showed up on their doorstep one day, asking if I could come live with them. They had no clue about what had gone done between Mom and me. Ruthann never had children of her own, but it was evident her yes decision supported a bigger plan. In between memories, events played out on the back of closed eyelids, forty years quickly edited into a short documentary of her loving kindness.

Balancing demands, also needing a decision was the timing for surgery. Abandoning my girls' team seemed higher on my doctor's priority list than mine. I voiced a strong desire to push all things robots and hospitals out so I could coach the girls across the finish line. They earned their berth, and I really wanted to show up and be present. Conversations ensued, rationales laid out. In short order, my medical team gave their blessing, surgery would be pushed out. *I will figure out a date and get back to you* all I could muster on the way out.

Life went on, but things weren't the same in the family after Ruthann's passing. Forty years of stepmotherdom ended in a flash. Routines changed, talks avoided the pain, family dealt as best we could, but I was different. The details of death and disease were getting sorted as time slowly passed. But misery loves company, so the party plodded on. Four weeks out from departure for club championships, the team was hit with a bit of bad news. Our best player partially tore a quadriceps training, would subsequently miss out on the biggest tournament of the year. We were all crushed. Two wins, eight losses reflected a team without its leader.

Third on the bitter pill list was preparing to transport my biological mother from Carmel, California to Oregon. Ironically, my cancer diagnosis only surfaced from seeking treatment for self-diagnosed depression. Two years, part-time living in cities one hundred miles apart, caretaking a mother battling dementia was emotionally consuming and hard to watch. Yet, with surgery on the horizon, physically unable to participate, I had to tap out. Gratefully, my sister stepped in for the hardest part of it all, another two years of tending to a mother in decline.

One weekend, I was hugging, saying goodbye, reassuring mom it was just a short-term visit to sister's house. Teardrops were extra-large and salty that morning. Everyone, including Alison in her faraway look, knew she wasn't coming back. Seven days hence, my first take on reality after a three-and-a-half-hour surgery, I woke up alone, disoriented, poking at the tubes coming out of me, fumbling to locate a pain button. It all seemed like a muddled, drug-induced dream.

It was my fourth surgical rodeo. Year-round training and competition were responsible for the first three. Four years playing NCAA D1 with an additional eight years training, playing internationally, five for the US National Team plus a three-year stint in Italian professional leagues. Toss in summer beach tournaments and some body part is bound to need a rest. Knee, shoulder twice, feet were the cut and close procedures. Herniated disks, broken fingers, sprained ankles, tweaked ligaments, stitches, cortisone shots, endless physical therapy the more drawn out annoyances.

All the above a fast track process compared to coming back from an internal reorganization. The prostatectomy busted my hump from just one ride. Stole the man purse right out of me while I was sleeping. No sports or serious training for a year? No mountain biking, no golf, no heavy lifting in the weight room? I hit the replay button, put on headphones and what the fuck hammered out to drums in my head. Not a happy camper.

It took time to settle in, but there was an upside to recovery. I rediscovered my healing process. No focus could be assigned to accomplishing much physically, so I found actual rest, a place of relative calm. The angst accumulated from all my outward attention on problems, challenges, personal loss began to subside. I worked back into a routine of walking contemplation, meditation, and writing. I started coming back 'in' after time looking out 'at' everything.

The better part of a year was spent wandering in the gray matter between my ears, gripping to make sense of things, all energy dedicated to looking 'at' things cognitively, constantly processing. In my days recuperating, the exhaustion in thought-form was visceral but also existed a growing desire to 'become' something again. To visualize and paint a new life portrait. Fresh canvas and new colors once again. Something that made me content, joyful. What a concept, right?

Reminders sprinkled throughout my writing, exclamation points, double underscores on many journal pages. I had the necessary tools, I just needed to empty out the toolbox, put everything out into the center of the room, figure out how those tools can serve in new ways. Consciously curious. Managing the mental chatter (spiritual Law of Substitution) was side by side understanding the emotions attached to said mental chatter. Wild winds of nothing important swirled and thrashed me about.

The reminder to focus inwardly, shift what I could control. Let the weather pass a voice reminded me.

The construct of "Platform 14" (offered up later in the book) had served me well treading back from an extended series of challenges, but also in crafting material and physical success. If it worked once, there was probably another teaching to uncover. However, in hopes of having one of those grand 'aha' moments, I knew with a tinge of angst, before that moment would manifest, some old internal code needed a re-write. From experience, rarely a smooth and straightforward process.

In the vein of relativity, a shift from the outer process to my inner process was prescribed. Becoming more disciplined, less emphasis and attention was placed on the subject of my 'at'tention. Embedded into my programming was the command for less grinding on the perceived scarcity in my reality. More emphasis placed on what my heartfelt intention would be going forward. What am I wanting to generate as a result of the time and work I am about to invest in this 'change'? From looking 'at,' to looking 'in.' What was the heart-spark that would power up another comeback?

Clarity arrived. Challenges across what I circled as the first phase were mental, physical and material things, issues. I laughed remembering how desperate I was in my prayer, my words, expressing desperation. But that perceived misery turned out to be only half of the whole. The follow-up phase looped more teachings, with different lessons. Loss, grieving love, sickness, health, how precise things are, how lucky we can be, timing, what does really matter. These were emotional, spiritual and energetic dwellings.

In my brain, lights flickered, gasses congealed, and then an explosion. Ah, fucking ha. It was a serious OMG moment. The pinnacle point to a new venture with intentions to help others had revealed itself. It was slowly gaining steam, refining, reshaping, recycling. For the first time in years, a heart-spark. How the spark would tinder a fire depended on me, but that was a channeling session for another day. A sense of renewed purpose followed by a twinge of urgency, the desire forming, not wanting to wait much longer, itching to begin the quest.

A byproduct of dealing with cancer, at least for me, was a definitive stance about how I recognized, then related to my own bullshit. I seemed to always bemoan people's bullshit factor, so following a reverse path, I looked in the mirror with a heightened awareness. I realized a lot about myself, what I wanted to attract and what I no longer wanted to attract or manifest, consciously or subconsciously. In performing, change is inevitable. Conversely, while in deep, structural change, performance is mandatory. The surgery not only took out my cancer, but it seemed to have also removed my fear.

Complaining, judging, ripping on other people, bemoaning the state of domestic and world affairs was perpetuating exact energies that needed shifting. How was I operating in the world in relationship to myself and others? What was, or was not, working in my life? What were the patterns of failed ventures, successful ones, even ones that didn't reap a harvest? Every file in my hard drive scrubbed for clues. Every time I found a charged file, breath and breathing, rhythm and flow, calmed me down to brace for the squall of emotion.

It started with the quiet observation of thoughts and random streams of mental commentary, what was coming out of my mouth generated by my brain. Then it shifted to assessing my emotional intelligence, how was I coping with primary negative emotions, fear, anger, shame, worry. Where was joy and happiness, let alone did I even comprehend how to create that state of feeling and being for myself?

Health and wellness took on new meaning. I refined my diet, going back to my love of cooking to construct a more vitalized approach to feeding and fueling my physical body. Having traveled around the world, my food tastes and preferences ranged wide and varied so out came the spices and cookbooks.

I went back into the kitchen, cooking with love for others. Sports Kitchen, fit needs fresh, was a digital platform I created from past training traditions. Plant-based nutritional regimens replaced animal products and all processed foods. From scratch or made fresh, the household freezer generally empty save ice, frozen fruit and plant protein for smoothies. Wholesome fuels, clean energy was the focus of everything put into my body.

Sidelined for months, enthusiasm for those first steps of aerobic activity woke up hibernating charges. Energy reserves perked up. A particular cadence was developing, a rhythm between fields of influence. Change was happening. That part was encouraging. Yet there was one realm of rebuild remaining. I had to refresh and reawaken a tired spirit. Something 'spiritual' in my life was missing. There were no rituals, circles, ceremonies. Sacred intention in sacrifice, that defining loop of service and self-awareness missing. The self-pity needed to shift.

But as I pondered what constituted my own heart-based thinking and doing, what was in place, what might be missing or not aligned, society and humanity kept drumming up things that seemed to lack anything resembling a spiritual approach to performance and transformation. Things in the world outside felt tense. A sense of societal angst stemming from developments stifling our heart-centers. Years of troubling media announcements marking additional tragedies, the follow-up tragedy seemingly more brutal than the prior event. Nothing short of shocking.

Shootings, killings, subway attacks, assassinations, suicide bombers, nationalism, genocide, all the light and dark sides of capitalism. Digital attacks on our privacy, data hacking, scams, false influencers, our routes, digital footprints, tracked, logged, mapped, ultimately sold to marketers. But don't stop there, friends. Opioids, Fentanyl, meth, heroin overdoses, suicides a dark backdrop to race and gender harassment, sexual misconduct, lies, exposes. Integrity, transparency, moral north compass, what's that? It's fake news.

Not to be a negative nelly, but the above shortlist doesn't even get us to US political dysfunction, or the thick wicket of Middle East-inspired drama. Soviets and Chinese pretty much smiling at our expense. Other world leaders snickering for different reasons. Living in a time where society has to absorb the possibility of a suitcase bomb or chemical device could blow in high-density population centers, or that a random, dark intentioned shooter might take another dozen lives hovers in the deep recesses of all.

Thank goodness we have our handhelds, email, and instant messaging to distract or remind. We can always resort to micro-dosing, induce more pleasure, ingest something to get us through another dull day. I don't need to remind you to look around and feel. There is very little accountability. It's ubiquitous. All in all, energetically sucking our light out, and in turn, our lightness of being. Not easy times my friends.

As if in a sequence of dance moves, the crescendo of collected angst, a prominent warning arrived. Digesting with disgust as I read the world's atomic scientists inched the Doomsday Clock two minutes to midnight. The read caused my stomach to knot up and puckered my sphincter. The clock had been at three minutes to midnight, moved from five minutes, a position stable for a decade. The primary influencers were the weather and the whackos on center stage.

The declaration was a hybrid warning concerning nuclear proliferation as well as climate change. The nuclear umbrella covers the dual variables of influence: known explosive material and its owners, those trying to manufacture, but also contamination from nuclear power (e.g.—Fukushima). Compact explosives were also referenced. The variables expand to then discuss world powers, threats, war, famine, fatwahs, and factions. Downright depressing.

The second category, climate change, was outlined with equal dismay. Things we know to some degree because if you are older than forty-five, you are experiencing different weather patterns from twenty years ago. Rising temperatures, melting glaciers, Greenland and the North Pole corridor melt possibly the most significant and daunting. Microplastics invading every layer and aspect of our oceans. Ecosystems are dying, drying up, getting gobbled up, or converted for greater income possibilities. Fracking, drilling, sucking, pumping, carbons, and emissions always the culprit. Consume, consume, consume. Throw away, throw away, throw away.

Put the cherry on top with ever-growing world population, greater need for renewable feedstocks and society's collective agenda gets more complicated. Species and sub-species are diminishing faster than predicted. Freshwater reserves are dwindling, but sea levels are rising (and warming). Weather is more intense, dramatic and disruptive. If we consider this earth a provider, then consider our Mother (Earth) is sick and showing signs of prolonged fever. Apparently, not enough of her children are aware she isn't feeling well.

Eleven months later, NOAA released their climate assessment report; the message was equally sour. We still have time, but the clock is ticking, loudly. The authors preaching a tipping point is upon us. If we don't change our relationship with our ecosystems, natural resources, animal environment, and habitats, things are going to change, and disappear, for the worse.

Domestically it took less than two years for POTUS to unravel many of our preservation and protection acts, pulling out of the Paris Agreement (UNFCCC), and still defying scientists and climatologists with logic bending statements. Duality on a global earth scale shows a reality our two polar extremes are melting down faster than we thought possible. Two minutes to ecological doomsday and no one batted a keyboard. As though we are to blame Mother Nature for going off the rails.

Reflecting on the world at large, there is a much denser, heavier vibration permeating relations. It's causing fragmentation. Everything that goes down is bigger and bolder than its predecessor. The cycle of escalation obviously has a ceiling point, but right now, there is a small sliver of space in which we can operate. Two minutes from that north point with no identifiable lightworkers SEAL Team founded and in operation. Just adopt the Bhutanese way, promote a gross national happiness index. Loving-kindness, what a concept.

Boo-hoo, but what to do? This is where all hit home for me. What I wanted to try, accomplish, become as I reconstructed. As the Sufi saying goes, it is the art of being and becoming. There is a map to guide us into a place of heart-sparked performance. Where the desire becomes a fire, not just cognitive combustion. It's the energetic spark from a resolution that crystallizes in the heart-center. It's a decision made with love. It's your truth, and upon that you act, with faith, well just because you know what that constitutes.

Instead of complaining and being judgmental, I employed the Law of Substitution, replacing a negative thought or expression with a more positive one. Feeling overwhelmed, emotional angst, in doubt or worry that one way of thinking is not going to move the collective needle enough, my emotional intelligence got a test. Shifting things I could control, from reactive to creative helped me stay lighter, not feel as heavy or burdened.

Physically and energetically I contracted a regimen of fitness, health, and wellness. It took ninety days just to prepare for real activity, slowly working up to revisit some of that gold medal mojo so fondly remembered. Muscle memory kicked in, but my lungs did not. Oxygenating body and brain assisted clear thoughts and thinking. A step of clarity. Tending to what and how I was eating, I returned to my hobby as a kitchen enthusiast, highlighting Sports Kitchen as a platform for performance, health, and wellness.

Employing 'sacred separation' helped clarify the purpose in all my attachments. Eating fresh, minding what pleasurable vices were being consumed or entertained helped delete the addiction file. Self-discipline magnified. Meditation sessions were calmer allowing a deeper drop into my body, feeling, sensing, being. I went back to my four-point routine with vigor, waiting for that one point to get clarified. For me, the point was spiritual. A laser of light projecting into a beautiful hologram. And yes, the vision was born.

However crazy, out there it seemed at the time, I refreshed efforts to finally write my follow up book. An intention delayed four years, but seemingly because I had a few more lessons to endure. I set out on my grand intention of weaving valuable information gleaned from successes and failures across decades of sports and life. How to garner forces and systems at our disposal to shape a much more powerful performance in the world, regardless of what that current expression looks like.

A direct current sparking change, growth, testing our emotional intelligence, we piece together physical truths and metaphysical teachings, allowing every practitioner access to answering those "why" questions. There is a map on how we can fearlessly cope with change, even in the face of not having the slightest clue where to begin, or with what intention. Methodology woven from physical successes and trials as an Olympic champion blended with the esoteric teachings, the metaphysical constants that are in play, how we access and leverage for our best and highest good.

Observing the self, how we operate mentally, emotionally, physically, and energetically, understanding each realm as a stand-alone system, great power is derived from integrating their points of truth. It's not enough to just cultivate a mindset of mental toughness, positivity. It's not enough to just say you are going to be loving-kindness, raise emotional intelligence. Singularly, each highly important, yet there are other systems keenly attached and involved.

On one basic level, it is about love, but ultimately this is a refined a-ha moment that emanates from the divine intelligence of our heart-center. This book is all about understanding what heart-sparked performance is. To understand the what, why, how, when and where, harnesses disparate sources of energy for greater performance in anything we choose to be or become.

Why you ask? Why does any of this matter? At the root of all matter, it's about time consciousness becomes more ingrained as a practice. How we relate, act, and create. I love myself and I love Mother Earth. I want to see her healthy and happier for our children. As a co-creator, I want to create to benefit the most people I can help or reach. For this to be a reality, progress towards the 'better' requires conscious change. Not an easy task.

THE 'HOW'

Any time we undertake a new venture there exists the
possibility the information necessary to answer our internal
query, 'how is this going to get done,' isn't tangible. Sometimes we
think we have a clue, enough relational experience to set off on a
new course, conquering, hammering with confidence. Yet, there
are those scenarios where we seize up, we haven't got a clue. We
don't know which first step is appropriate. Conquering how to do
anything blends both the constants and variables involved.

Sports provides plenty of objective examples. There are
constants that must be observed, respected, whether you agree
with them or not. First, you must make the team. There are skills
you are expected to have to compete for a roster spot. Technical
discipline must be exhibited and applied. There are constants
in the structure: offense, defense, positions, plays, tactics, trajectory, time and tenacity. Variables would be the range of skills
across all players competing, different abilities, shortcomings,
and strengths. Speed, coordination, height, reflexes all must be
factored.

In a corporate or professional setting, there might be more
variables than constants. Layers of management, chains of command, products, malfunctions, redundancy, desires of different
departments, politics, every layer of senior management jockeying
for something. There is always a game within the game.

All said, in any situation, there is a circle containing 'you'
and then there is another circle encompassing, the 'it,' 'goal' or

'success.' Be it having to physically accomplish something, or the esoteric work of personal growth, changing our ways. There exists a dynamic between two separate entities encompassing the objective and the subjective.

Before any 'how' can be analyzed, learned, absorbed, and executed, there is a key starting point. Doing your basic home-work, assess as much about all sides involved as best as possible. Observing without commentary, gathering factoids, assembling what you think you see, about yourself, and the other entity involved. Some things you know more certainly than others. There's 'you' and there's 'it.' Each entity requires study before you can construct a game plan.

There is very much a process of 'know thyself' in fine-tuning our performances. We have hardwiring, inherent gifts, attributes bestowed on us at birth; we have our operating system, software, our program code, different applications for how we relate, how we hear things, how we influence, shape things under our control, nature vs nurture. All of humanity embodies this. Each of us swimming around in the same five operating systems that comprise life. Our minds, emotions, physical bodies, energy/life current, and the etheric spiritual, the divine.

Any quest begins with contemplation, observation of known aspects and variables. If I am acting as a facilitator, serving as a guide to another place or experience, the first tone I am looking to tune is encouraging a seeker mindset. Imparted would be things to look for along the way, unique vistas, unusual formations, perspectives from varying angles, elevations. What do you see, and what thoughts does it stir up? What do you feel in your being alongside the other sensory information?

In my coaching work, when an assessment is presented, clients quickly voice *so how does this actually go down?"* Since verbal or word descriptions will only take a mind so far, implementing visualization exercises is often utilized as a sound tone-setter. Encouraging the creation of an imaginarium (the make-believe space where one constructs an imaginary vision to their standards, wishes, and desires). The power of imagination, thinking outside our basic box, squelching mental chatter and judgment serves to raise our spirit through whimsy, fantasy, the potentiality in 'what if.' There is freedom because things shape in mind's eye as you so desire. This is positive.

Stepping into a role as facilitator, breathe in a few examples by letting yourself wander through an imaginary experience like you are participating. The purpose here is to foster a mindset. Pretend I speak to you as a guide, three hypothetical protagonists in three imaginary plays, docent, park ranger, and a specialty skills coach.

The first scene to be constructed in your imaginarium places you in a world-famous museum with a very experienced art docent. In their roles, docents spend many hours touring majestic artifacts, renowned masterpieces, works of art spanning centuries, observing, learning, studying. An appreciator of art, the job as a guide requires exploring the subject matter in detail, with hundreds of visitors around you, or in the quiet hours post lockdown in a solitary visit.

Gazing at a masterpiece, the docent provides threads of information about how the object came to be, the genesis, where the artist was in his/her life, the joy, the suffering. Most likely it will be suggested that the viewer looks at a specific angle, then a different perspective, possibly with different lighting. Highlighting specific elements, places of structural genius in the art, the possibilities of an interpretive whim when viewing. Studying intently, coming full circle in a viewing walkabout, new information, new perspectives command new respect in your relationship with that object.

If you are a lover of nature, construct an imaginary journey to an outdoor place of magnificence you have dreamed of visiting, complete with a veteran park ranger as your personal guide. You may be asked what you would enjoy exploring, possibly old-growth forest, a raging river, a majestic waterfall. Each exploration, in and of itself, an expansive experience. Moving, raw power, decades in place, you feel the grandeur. There is what you see and the depth of what you feel.

The sounds, the moisture, the air, the sights, the smells. The grandfathers and grandmothers of nature it is said. Hundreds, thousands of years around you. Maybe the side notes provide historical perspectives, who came before, how was the place used, why is it so unique, why is it such a wonder to have this ecosystem in place, thriving.

Facilitating a shift in experience for a visitor could be to view from a particular vista or listening to the wind blow through a grove of pines, whooshing or whispering. The geology of time embedded in a cliff face, the icy chill, and pureness of rushing stream water. You sit on a rock, in a beautiful place, feeling, sensing, releasing. You can feel something you can't quite describe in word form. The impact on your being becomes visible in your face, your smile, your spirit. Someone helped you see someplace with different perspectives. Powerful.

As a professional go-getter with a strong desire to rapidly ascend the corporate ladder you open yourself to specialty skills coaches. Life, business, sales, or sports. You are under someone's watch where the promised product is to advance your work, income, or life goals. An experienced teacher sets about working their magic, establishing new dots, asking you to connect these new dots, overseeing the phases where your process succeeds or derails, and how.

What are you now, what do you wish to become? Does criticism or rejection trigger a shame response? Is there a visceral physical reaction you detect when words are received 'the wrong way'? Analyzing your verbiage, tells, twitches, takeaways from the other side, the monologue, the posturing. You are forced out of self-centeredness to consider the impact of forces beyond your control.

Regardless of example, each journey involves acts of consciousness. Pure focus and observation of external experience and the internal responses generated in our being. Consciousness, as I emphasize in this book, is developing greater (self) awareness through quiet observation. The mindful study of the 'at' and 'in,' balancing what grabs our attention with what intentions are in play. Mindfulness.

Consciousness has this rap that it is some intangible concept or dimension. Basic consciousness is expanding one's range of awareness. This could be your physical environment or more esoteric considerations such as what comes up while meditating. It could be raising one's frequency or peeling back layers, healing as we tend to our emotional wounds. But it starts with quiet assessments.

If you are talking, you can't listen effectively. The first part of how to do anything begins with heightened self-awareness, observing and identifying all parts and pieces possible. Being mindful of what it means to elevate consciousness. The second phase becomes tuning out static, distractions that will ultimately come around to push us off the path. Thus, basic mindfulness towards expanding consciousness becomes vital in progressing our performances or engaging change.

Executing with a high level of integrity, work-life balance, personal growth work are multi-dimensional events. Of course, there are causes and effects. Our purported happiness squelched by outside forces. But the waters run deeper. Any path for any vocation initiated requires a similar schematic to produce success. Most of our focus is placed on the tangible, physical pieces. We apply force and expect progress. If it doesn't shape to personal expectations, frustration, exasperation, resentment start brewing. Whatever our five senses generate, the relational database of mind continues to grind. Dissonance grows. Here we cultivate mindfulness.

In performance is a transformation of self. We are different the farther up the mountain we climb. It is not all about force equaling progress. it's about how we relate to various chunks of the climb, what is confronted on the path, and how ultimately we perceive and mentally comment on the challenge. Relativity, shifting perspectives opens us to different stimuli, experiences, and hidden caves to explore. If there is a need to elevate what has been a string of average performances, new methods must be discovered and applied.

Executing in performance or initiating change is a multi-part process. Co-creation does not start or finish in the mental realm. Of course, we need to create positive thoughts, speech, and behavior, but there are other systems which have profound effects on thoughts and thinking. There are fundamental, universal concepts, then advanced teachings.

Advanced learning incorporates the discipline of mindfulness to observe what happens when 'systems' are not in balance. Again, a formula with variables and constants. What happens to our minds, thoughts, and perspectives when these processes are subject to extreme duress? A novice practitioner will most likely notice the negative chatter telling us to stop, forcing us to debate why we are even doing this. The ego steps in to be heard, loudly. Learning is accelerated when we cipher is this reminder pain, or portal pain, a fear painted door needing to be opened and then closed once on the other side.

Early-stage work in the 'how' to create, discover, or shift must integrate all systems. How? Identifying and understanding the basic functioning and processes of the five realms humans embody is critical. Each realm (referred to as Circles of Consciousness) has attributes and functions which require calibration and conscious management to ensure positive vibration output. While most hover around mind, body, and spirit, emotions and our energy grid are paths less often explored.

Variables, the unknown, chaos, luck, timing, perspective, how we think, how we feel merges into how we deal, how we relate. External and internal signs, signals, stimuli bombard an ecosystem which ultimately must be in balance to yield maximum efficiency. Conversely, identifying processes which have kept us out of balance, always in a state of reactivity (drama) are equally important to identify, manage.

Humankind, as sentient beings, has broad operating consistency. We live and cultivate on a planet which is a system of integrated ecosystems. Mother Earth is a living and producing organism. This system is subject to physical law (science) and natural law (metaphysics). The path this book takes is a journey where consciousness is emphasized, and at points, forced into practice. Systems with constants and variables. The hope, a concept introduced becomes a conviction, via experience. Everything is connected.

There are constants we must heed. Because these constants cover aspects of physical law, their influence is acknowledged by science. Their role in how we grow as human beings philosophically debated. When you want to figure out how something works, start with taking it apart, inspect the primary components individually, understand how and where they are connected. Observe, clean, polish, lubricate and reassemble.

As it relates to this journey by JR, the opening exercise is to digest the essences of five life constants which are present and in-play across each circle of consciousness. Concepts and components embedded in duality, energy, force, geometry, and balance are ever-present influencers and significant metaphors when applied to a performance schematic. Esoteric yet applicable across all chapters to follow. Five constants will influence the properties of our five circles of consciousness and chat about the 'How' will shape accordingly.

THE 'WHEN' AND 'WHERE' . . .

. . . is the here and now.

Tick tock goes the clock.

The external voices, writers, scientists, panels, commissions, are generating more chatter. *Look what climate change is doing.* The clock is ticking. The pressure is on. If you are not yet convinced, things are out of balance. What needs to be 'solved' first and by when are big questions.

If you subscribe to the proverb, as within, so without/ as above, so below, isn't it logical to add consciousness to the mix of influencers? If our stuff on the outside is distorted, chaotic, challenging, unbearable or just plain frustrating for the umpteenth time, it's time to recognize change is necessary.

Don't just push the reset button and go about your business the way you have been. Get outside your comfort zone and initiate the exploration which will spark a fire of desire to get it done. This time, with higher applications of conscious evaluation, set the stage to discover your heart-spark. With practice, you won't leave home without it.

FIVE CONSTANTS IN CONSCIOUSNESS

Duality, Energy, Force, Geometry, and Balance

DUALITY

In Eastern philosophy, there is greater emphasis on the concept of duality than in western teachings. The classic Yin/Yang symbol is a whole, balanced by opposites. Yin/Yang: Two halves that together complete wholeness. Yin ("shady side") and Yang ("sunny side") are also the starting point for change. When something is whole, by definition, it's unchanging and complete. When you split something into two halves—Yin/Yang, it upsets the equilibrium of wholeness. Both halves are chasing after each other as they seek a new balance with each other.

Yin Yang is the concept of duality forming a whole. We encounter examples of Yin and Yang every day. As examples: night (Yin) and day (Yang), female (Yin) and male (Yang). The symbol Yin Yang is called the Taijitu. Light/dark, positive/negative, matter/ anti-matter, quarks/antiquarks, up above and down below, x's and o's, 0's and 1's. Opposing forces coexisting in balance and stability. In each opposite, a piece of the other.

Alongside duality there is the topic of dualism. Typically, humans are characterized as having both a mind (nonphysical) and body/brain (physical). Dualism is the view that the mind and body both exist as separate entities. Human beings are material objects. We have weight, solidity, and consist of a variety of solids, liquids, and gases. However, unlike other material objects (e.g.— rocks) humans can form judgments and reason their existence. In short, we have 'minds.'

Descartes argued that the mind interacts with the body at the pineal gland. This form of dualism or duality proposes that the mind controls the body, but that the body can also influence the otherwise rational mind, such as when people act out of passion.

If you can resonate with a premise in divinity, that we are all the same light, embodied in an array of containers, the same perspective can be applied to any dynamic we encounter. However much we want to soapbox our beliefs, duality presents a reflection, the positive and the negative. There exists somewhere out there, like-kind matter or compatible charges that will bond. Small or large, discernible by eye or not, anything is possible.

Because of duality, dual realities exist. Not parallel, dual. You can always become something else, something different, something more positive. Your expression is never one and done. If it is, just a choice. You and the person right next to you are going for the same prize. Your preparation and level of readiness is your reality, not the other persons. There are dual realities, yours and theirs.

For as many variables processed, you must presume your competitor has done equal work. Relative success or failure in life is not graded on a curve. Objectives, needs, baseline requirements, constants, and variables. For many, life is a game of survivor and you don't really know who is going to help or hinder you. Thus, you must exist to the best of your primal powers. Hunt or be hunted about as dualistic as it gets.

For everything we know about our abilities, capabilities, also exists a reality where there are better/worse (above or below your level) when comparing to yourself. Personal growth work involves bettering our dynamics, towards positive/constructive and away from negative/deconstructive. In competition, we must better others to succeed. It's not an ego thing; it is what it is, you win or lose. Most points accumulated you get a trophy. While anything is possible, win or lose is binary.

Metaphysically, duality imparts clues when dealing with other people and personalities. It is said that when others display behavior, words, or attitudes that cause us to react negatively (judgment, righteousness, shame) that core element of behavior is a reflection of what we need to address in our own psyche.

If you hate when people act certain ways, it truly annoys you is quite possibly the shadow energy of a subconscious quality embedded in your personality you don't like. This aspect of duality operates as a reflection, merely providing an opportunity for consciousness to be engaged and observed in how we relate to others and our self. Situations and people can be mirrors to see something else.

When we can engage situations pushing our mind to hold space for the many realities that are not our own, greater respect is developed. This, in turn, fosters a practice of detachment, which is an act of intentionally not dedicating energy to a vibration, positive or negative. It is what it is. Because practicing detachment requires consistent self-discipline, a positive energy pattern builds, diminishing the focus on the negative. That which we water grows.

One master key is embracing and leveraging the metaphor embedded in duality: concentration (creating) on a positive 'charge,' versus reacting to a negative 'charge.' Creative or reactive. The offense must execute in the face of the defense, and vice versa. Part game plan, part perspective, part performance. Embrace that which you can create in any moment to confront any challenge while respecting where you divert energy and resources reacting. Managing situations, persons, challenges, trials, consumes time and energy. If managing situations feels like all you do, some 'things' are not in balance.

Train, sell, manage or lead. Eventually, you get to the championship round or see progress reflected in your compensation. Maybe you are a top producer, the number one seed going into playoffs then get jacked. Maybe you have just bonked, hit the proverbial wall. Some yearning, some itch you can't quite stifle. Management hierarchies, power trips and control plays, politics. So many things going back channels it can be hard to know all the variables. Take away categorical separations labeled sports, work, relationships or politics. Try the perspective life is a spiritual sport, see what shifts in how you relate.

Comebacks, the out-of-nowhere upset, flops, failures, stories for the ages. Injuries, sacrifices, blown chances, bad apples. It becomes a large collection of opposites all trying to squeeze into the same space. But we must keep our cool, not panic, not be overwhelmed with the unknown. Sometimes it is meant to be, sometimes not so much. Deal with it. Embrace your intentions and yearnings will be eventually satisfied with answers.

The main takeaway from this constant is there is always hope. Anything can happen, and everything is connected. Separate, yet integrated, when we act consciously, we are mindful and more efficient of how and what we are co-creating.

ENERGY

Atoms show energy can be observed. Protons and neutrons are the standard starting points. Standing and staring at an individual, plant, rock or animal, it is hard to identify the entity's energy. We hold space knowing there is energy in all matter, but can you see ghosts, auras, energy fields? Can you hold onto an ancient rock to feel it's accumulated wisdom over time?

Some can, most don't. To attune energetically requires training our inner quiet. We must cipher stimulus and begin dropping in, so to speak. Energy is stable or unstable, a positive charge or a negative charge. Organically our physical bodies operate in a closed system, energies which bump and balance. Beyond physical appearances, there is a composing set of energies which constitute our life current. All must thrive within a certain range of conditions or systems begin to shut down.

Protons, neutrons, electrons, quarks, anti-quarks, matter, anti-matter joined in structure, balancing forces. Fission unleashes energy by breaking atoms apart; fusion by compressing those same atoms. Situations, people, words, actions, positive energy can hold situations together while negative energy (or divergent energy) usually blow things apart. The animosity in vitriolic words is palpable, yet so is the connection in a good hug.

In the grand loop of things via the Law of Return smack comes back with a whack. You can't map it, but you believe in energetic exchanges.

There is energy in every personal dynamic, team structure. People attract (vibe), repel (don't like) or offset, meaning there is no charge one way of the other. There is latent energy which can also erupt. Discussing energy is esoteric because it isn't something we taste, touch, hear, or see. Could be a headache, a knot in your shoulder, a cranky back. You know it's something, somewhere, but rarely pay attention to tuning in, checking in on your grid.

As with duality, there is a scientific/physical discussion and there is the esoteric/metaphysical side of categorizing energy.

Meridians, chakras, nodes, nadis, nervous systems are the throughways and checkpoints which serve as the body's electrical grid. The system in whole has connectivity which must be monitored. Body temperature when over one hundred degrees begins to affect related organs and nervous system functions. Heat, running hot requires energetic effort to counterbalance. Too cool and things start to slow down, hibernate. Making sure our energy is not stuck, blocked, but flowing efficiently is generally not a process of conscious management. We breathe all the time, yet don't celebrate our next breath.

Like the hum of an active overhead power line, our subtle energy system emits a vibration. If your energetic body produces a musical note, the hum vibrates to a frequency, the range bass/low to alto/high. When people talk about a need to fine-tune, tweak, this involves altering a core vibration. We strive to emit a different frequency, consciously engineered. Experiencing jitters, agitation, feeling angst can reflect blocked energy somewhere in the circuits. In more acute scenarios depression and anxiety reflect in high blood pressure, less efficient brain functioning, low energy levels.

Our whole system produces and consumes energy, literally and figuratively. Feedstocks, both organic (animal/plant-based) and inorganic (artificial/processed) are providers of energy as we digest, assimilate, absorb proteins, carbs, fats, and liquid. What we consume as fuel burns clean or dank, depending on how it resonates enzymatically. However, consuming can constitute things not in solid or liquid form. Words, actions, trauma, negative energy we don't need to see, hear or feel, puts pressure on energy transfer stations in the body. These are energetic impressions consumed via absorption.

Energy is tapped situationally, hugging, fighting, exerting, crying, in memories, visions, and longings. Emotional energy is triggered while you are patiently waiting, the feel-good anticipation of a heart-warming, home-cooked meal, fresh and fantastic. Think about the feeling in your body, the smile on your face, events of the day quickly forgotten. Yum energy.

Shift to imagining one of those, in your grille monologues from a superior, peer, partner, friend or foe. Lighting you upside down and sideways, obviously not happy with you (or themselves for that matter). You can feel the force behind the words, the anger. You can feel the words blow your body wall. It oozes through the skin, gives you goosebumps, makes your stomach seize, breathing halted. Yuck energy.

Prayers, hopes, desires, our intentions, our motivation, heartfelt wants and needs all are activated by the longing, the aching, the surrender of one's self for the betterment of another. Powerful spiritual energy is generated by acts of sacrifice, being in service. There is creative power inherent in ideation, visualization, and imagery. The stirring excitement one feels and applies while looking to connect disparate thoughts, ideas, or concepts.

There is energy embedded in our emotions. Anger is chaotic. Fear is frozen. Worry produces distortion. Grief is damp and dense. Joy, on the other hand, is high octane energy. On a spiritual level, we come to understand energy as divine or destructive, light or dark.

Through our physical body, we feel the energy from clean, energetically vibrant food sources. Good nutrition supports cellular vibrancy. The kosher, blessed, or organically raised and treated with the energy of love. We can raise the vibration of what we put into our machine with energetic intention. Praying over or before a meal serves such a purpose. We continuously reaffirm that hugging is an energetic feel good, getting punished is a not so much.

HEART-SPARKING PERFORMANCE

Meditation, like quantum physics, deals with energy unrestricted by the constrictions of space and time. It enhances our understanding of 'potential' not be constricted and hinged by sociological and psychological limitations we have set upon ourselves, allowing us to be more in tune with space and time as well as feeling somehow *beyond* space and time. Generally, breath-based sequences are prime pathways in the practice of discernment.

Discerning positive and negative energies, internally and externally, is equally important as is learning how to keep your personal energy levels flowing. In sports or professional performance, one learns what to foster, what to protect against. Experience shows performance can be influenced, positively or negatively, depending on how your wired system responds under duress.

Energy garnered and leveraged, or dispersed via fragmentation can be the difference between the mountaintop or massive meltdown. Remember, we are daily tenders of the body-mind interchange. With greater awareness of inherent energies, we can sharpen focus, fine-tune attention essentially creating a useable laser beam. Power up and point. In the right hands, a highly effective tool.

FORCE

Applied force goes both ways. Moving things to our advantage requires proverbial force. Force = Mass x Acceleration. Freeing ourselves, separating from applied force could be life or death. There are torrential forces of nature, compassionate forces in mankind. Common perspective on a physical plane is that force equals progress. Too much force and one side deconstructs. Too little force and we get stuck in the two steps backward, one step forward retreat.

Force in spiritual terms does not relate to progress so to speak. The essence of intentions in any action, prayer or vision of creation is an energetic force. The energy generated in our heart, love (or hate) can be described as a force. Belief, faith is considered a spiritual force which portends the proverb love can move mountains. Is a tangible force more powerful than etheric force? If you pray are you going to move the boulder out of your way? Discounting leverage and gravity, probably not. But have you ever prayed for someone's miracle to arrive? I did, and now I no longer pray to move boulders.

Watching a bat splinter from a sizzling pitch, a hockey player getting slammed into the plexiglass, a body being thrown back in contact, benches clearing. Whack. It just sounds like it hurt. Maybe the reflection of force, merely a cool smile and sizzling stare after posting a career-high to bury your opposition. No noise, no throwdowns, no trash talking. Pure performance. In the eyes of the sports gods, equally forceful.

In physical form, force is present in everyday living. Per Newton's Laws of Motion, mathematically force can be calculated by the equation, $F= mv2/r$. The most ubiquitous references to how we relate to force are centrifugal and centripetal. We know centrifugal force as we ride a merry-go-round, turn a corner while driving, or watch the washing rumble in spin mode.

Centripetal is closely related. The relevant example of centripetal force would be an amusement park ride where a spinning room at a specific speed will pin the rider against the wall without needing floor support. (Complicating conceptions: centripetal force is defined as an actual force, whereby centrifugal is defined as an 'apparent' force).

Taught in most sports training regimens, is that force equals progress. But in life situations, often our encounters are more push/pull. Our physical body interacts with force differently than does our mind, emotions and energy field. Spiritual force, light and dark, is a more advanced and refined conversation. My intention is not to dismiss the precept force equals progress, but reflected back through personal experiences in high-level sports competition, juxtaposed to periods of complete fasting in sacred sacrifice, there is a creative/reactive dynamic where force is involved.

How we apply force and how we relate to force directed at us is where maturity in our game helps us progress. This embraces the concept of efficiency and leverage as we toggle in and out of applying force, or when dealing with an opposing force. Force embraces elements of constants one and two, duality and energy.

On the universal scale, there are five levels/types of force:

1. *Physical Force*
    The most 'rudimentary' and least efficient. In muscle contractions, more heat than torque is generated. Sports science has helped refine strength and conditioning models, increasing yield while helping to reduce injuries through cross-functionality, stretching, nutrition, speed/ footwork, and jump performance. Embraces Newton's second law of motion: F=ma.

2. *Gravity (leverage)*
    Gravitational constant is an empirical physical constant. Tricky in that we can't mentally process the math instantaneously. We don't think about it, we are used to it. Bottom line is how high/far can you jump, how long can you hover? Leverage does not have the same construct as a physical force because there is no output of force generated by the density of mass being leveraged.

3. *Prana (Pranic Energy)*
    Prana is a Sanskrit word literally meaning 'life force'—the invisible bio-energy or vital energy that keeps the body alive and maintains a state of good health. The Japanese call this subtle energy Ki, the Chinese, Chi, the Greeks, Pneuma, Hindu the Shakti. Polynesian culture, it is known as Mana, in Hebrew, Ruah, 'Breath of Life.' In Yoga manipulation of our north/south energy grids is referred to as working with the Kundalini. In Native American traditions, pranic energy is the fifth direction, the heart-center.

4. *Imagery*
    Energy embedded in thoughtform is a potent force. The act of combining (At)tention and (In)tention to paint a mental image is ideation, idea-sparking action, creation. Concepts of manifestation, intuition, motivation, imagination, crea- tivity all embrace this potent force. There are no boundaries to dreaming, fantasizing. Here we can guide a 'higher self'

to see, trusting all systems will shape to the construct in mind's eye. The energetic paradox embodied, is seeing-believing, or believing-seeing?

5. *Spiritual Intention (motivation)*
   Energy concentrated in the heart, the laser beam consisting of (At)tention and (In)tention is considered the most potent force. When desire is colored with knowledge of self, understanding selfless service, the practice of sacred sacrifice, the motivation to do something for the best and highest good of all involved is a spiritual platitude. Love can move mountains.

The sound construction of anything is about supporting energies and distributing force. Force as a constant in consciousness work requires dualistic practices. When and how to apply force, and what kind of force, to discerning forces not for your best and highest good and learning how to defend against, deflect or diffuse.

Paying greater attention to energies we consume and produce facilitates intentional applications of various types of force we use as we go about our day. Broad examples that become metaphors later. If you are a lover, not a hater, one finds protection against negative hate forces is important to wellbeing. If you find you are 'gripping too hard' grappling with a debilitating situation, let go of the handlebars. Gripping produces fear energy. Letting go dissipates that negative force.

Geometry

The word *geometry* comes from the Greek words *Geos* meaning 'earth' and *Metron* meaning 'to measure,' which together literally translates as the 'measuring of the earth' or 'earthly measurements,' an art which was traditionally restricted to the priesthood.

Arcs, angles, lines, vectors, circles, squares, pyramids, polyhedrons. From the straightforward one-hundred-meter dash to opening up the right side of a defensive line, ball movement, slicing, swinging and striking, how we read, relate and realign is critical to creating an advantage. The ability to relate to geometrical structures in space and time is 'on the fly' engineering. Shapes, lines, angles, how an individual relates to his/her environment, respecting its geometry is a process of increasing awareness: self-awareness of your surroundings, all the variables in action.

We exist vis-a-vis a bounty of geometrical relationships. Competition venues are elliptical, circles, squares or diamonds. Buildings are most often connected right angles, rectangular or square. Most balls are round. Pools, tracks, courts, roads, and bridges have their geometry, curves, and elevations. The great pyramids and majestic cathedral spires point to the heavens, three dimensional. The pouring of foundations in construction composes geometric grids, platforms. Mother Earth is a source and a resource, a circle, an ecosystem. Galaxies, planets and stars energies, geometries all constantly studied. The science of shape in structure and motion.

We create an arching shot, have to carve a line down a mountain, or work a gap, wiggle an angle. Are we trying to get to the corner office, or springboard into another, higher-paying job? Is your path straight ahead or circuitous? We go a long way or the short way. We talk in straightforward or roundabout ways. Stacking, spreading, a triangle offense, box and one, man to man, woman to woman, hand to hand, foil against foil, mind versus mind. it's about the relationship to shapes, stationary and in motion.

In some spiritual traditions, the crafts of light versus dark is represented by circles and squares. Circles are associated with light work; square geometry utilized in the dark arts. Sacred drawings, mandalas all reflect geometric balance. Our physical alignment is north, south, east, and west. There is the up above, and down below, lines, grids, boundaries, and barriers. Two dimensions turning three dimensional maybe to a fifth dimension? Numbers, geometric order; nature, abstract perfection in balance.

Everything we relate to has a form and a function. Beyond what we all learned as basic geometry in high school, there exists a transcendent level all things geometric. Beauty in nature is amplified by symmetry. The balancing patterns in flowers, colors, shells, rock formations, tree limbs inspire our spirit. A passionfruit flower is mesmerizing because of its geometric beauty. It's sacred for what it shows us. There is sacred geometry.

The synchronicity of the universe is determined by certain mathematical constants which express themselves in the form of patterns and cycles in nature. These displays of mathematical and geometric constants are confirmation that certain proportions are woven into the very fabric of nature. Nature's expression and everything around us, are the product of the delicate balance between chaos and order. Enter civilizations contributions and here we are facing dramatic change.

Historically, many civilizations applied geometry in construction with an intention toward the divine. Outside of natural perfection, mankind has applied metaphor in sacred geometry which has left clear geometric fingerprints in their greatest constructions. Churches, cathedrals, pyramids, tombs, places of worship, places of mystery all exhibit sacred geometry in their base engineering. Minoans, Greeks, Egyptians, Sumerians, Indus Valley, Chinese, Phoenicians, Celtic, Native Americans, other indigenous cultures had cultural artistic expressions that were constructed with sacred intentions.

However we encounter life's geometry, its role as a consciousness constant is that it provides building blocks we assemble or take apart if we don't like our finished project. Take the example of the circle, a base component for other shapes, can be seen using what is known as the vesica pisces. Starting with the vesica pisces, one can produce an equilateral triangle, hexagon, pentagon, square, and so on and so on . . .

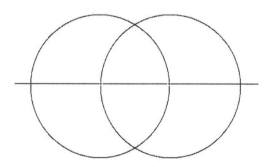

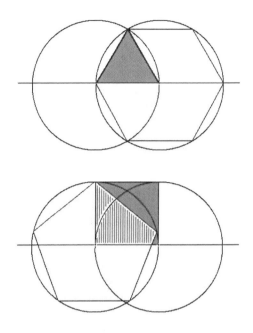

BALANCE

All systems in nature strive towards equilibrium. Extremes create stress, and structural stress leads to structural failure. Balance, when systems are in a state of equilibrium, defines proper rhythm and flow. Balance implies harmony. Where and how this influences our perspective as we walk the path is embracing that balance, while we are in motion, thinking and doing, is representative of our flow, our personal equilibrium.

Balance and perfection are normal states of being, not abnormal. Thus, in infinity, continuity through space and time reflects balance but also the range of extremes. These can again be positive or negative conditions. Extreme force applied or received causes unbalancing, whereby the unbalancing of any situation is a negative influence, a reaction. In shaping towards balance, there is also a force in counterbalancing.

In the metaphysical or conceptual sense, balance is used to mean a point between two opposite forces that is desirable over purely one state or the other, e.g.—metaphysical Law of Chaos. The law by itself being overly-controlling, chaos being overly-unmanageable, balance being the point that minimizes the negatives of both.

Balance, the fifth constant, is a state of desired being for the basic properties in our mind, body, spirit realm emphasizing an even keel, energetically. Keeping an open mind is counterbalancing 'judgment.' Managing emotions that have a debilitating effect on performance, mental and physical, is a balancing act. A positive mindset can be quickly hampered by disruptive emotional energies, lingering pain, or unhealthy food. Input affects output. Too much sugar and we experience a 'crash.' Too little water and our core temperature rises, cellular activity slows.

Effort, concentration, a little bit of productive anxiety are always necessary for work, progress, accomplishing anything. Defining what 'drives' us in our actions is part of 'knowing thyself.' Being mindful implies cognitive understanding that at some point, systems strive for balance. We must maintain balance to perform optimally over time. If we are not fine-tuning the machine, taking time out to balance, recalibrate, there is a risk of malfunction. This is where conscious control is lost and a gasket is blown. We must do our best daily to strive for operational balance.

Balance, equilibrium reflects in duality. If there is a balance in the micro, the macro mirrors that balance. While there is a system of balance within each realm, creative versus reactive, the five circles of consciousness also need to balance as a collective: mental and emotional feed off each other as the pair on a teeter-totter; energetic and physical are always integrating the down below and the up above. Spiritually, we strive to balance earthly and heavenly.

When striving for peak performance, rational beings should respect that exerting personal will, constantly shaping things around personal needs, serving up an agenda, reflects billions of identical actions humanity plays out daily. Unnecessary force, covert pressure tactics such as manipulation, bullying, leveraging, squeezing something out, creates a disturbance, minor or major, throwing systems out of balance.

Whether particle physics or a metaphysical quest to fine-tune your system, with the list of responsibilities we must execute daily, 'balance' is what we seek. The metaphors are many. Balancing our personal environment requires balancing two parts which make the whole. As within, so without.

THE PATH

A t this exact point, in the here and now, we all have paths we are walking or seeking out. If you are here, still reading, there are probably reasons. I won't pry or nit-pick. Doesn't have to be acknowledged to others. But if there is something more you want out of life, or with your life, you will continue into this work. Full disclosure: it is a path that must be walked, tried, experienced, not judged before you fully appreciate the destination point.

As we gather our conceptual necessities prior to embarking, tone-setting has been the objective. Mentally prepping, hopefully, excited to understand what is behind all this talk about consciousness, mindfulness, and performance, it's time to crystallize a personal intention. To accomplish this, I suggest the following relatively brief imaginary exercise. Laid out in front of you covering edge to edge of your coffee table are books holding your entire life story to this exact point.

Whatever your path has been up to this point, savory success or succinct suffering, I ask you to separate from all that you have filed away. Without judgment as to good or bad, just see your life story laid out in front of you. From early to current, stretch those books and chapters out left to right across the table. Just stare at all that is written and done. It might be covered in a trilogy, or possibly strung out across twelve hardcover beauties. Take it all in.

After absorbing the imaginary visual, stand up and step away. In your imaginarium, whatever that construct is for you, make it a separate entity. Literally separate from your story to the best of your ability. Get up and walk away. Keep all that you believe is you and detach, soon free to observe from a different perspective. No grinding, no remorse, no regrets.

Regardless of where you fall on the range of relative success or failure on your current path, regardless of great successes or great trials, the ask is to construct a perspective of absolute gratitude (a thank you) for literally everything you have undergone to this point in life. To this exact minute. Disregarding the ego's input, quell the chatter and force your perspective to see everything written being grateful. Yes, I understand this is a big ask.

Gratitude for the teachings learned in the trials. What you learned from your successes, and your perceived failures. If there is a negative storyline in place, convince yourself to seek out a silver lining. Every situation has one. In the chapters of our stories, we remember commentaries long forgotten or skimmed over the first read. Even in the darkest of days, with hindsight, you should be able to look back and identify something that was a blessing. If you are happy, be grateful. If not, find a way to be grateful for something.

Hovering in this energy, pick a story, a memorable event (positive or negative) and revisit. This time, separate any emotional charge, happiness or hatred, and reconstruct in your mind's eye. Imagine the duality of the situation you endured, what you thought you knew, maybe how things could have gone differently. Maybe in hindsight reflection, there is a fragment you can glean to see things differently.

There are those that preach all has been for a reason. Fated they would say. But since anything is possible and everything is connected, take a moment to sit, breathe, command an attitude of being grateful for something in the memory. Even if it is a stretch, pour gratitude over your head and just get wet.

While in this process of incubation, bring into your conscious mix the philosophy of each constant presented: duality, energy, force, geometry, and balance. One by one, mix each constant into your bowl of gratitude and contemplate how each may have operated over the course of your imagined story. In the interest of time, maybe pick one constant and overlay over your storyline. Where could things have been different, on your part and from the other entity?

• • •

Any path is a process. A path exploring consciousness and why it is important to high-level performance is by no means a straight line. Rarely do we find ourselves able to smoothly go from point A to point B. The more responsibility we have, or take on, magnifies the processes that must be managed. If we dropped our performance into a body of water, there would be ripples, but how far would they travel, how impactful is that body of performance on its surroundings? Science would like to measure it; Philosophy would like to debate it.

Due to the pure volume of processes, signals, energies a community or a society produce, actions and reactions, cause and effect, often, paths are not linear. Winding, turning, rising, falling, or improvising because a portion of the path got washed out, everything encountered on the path is variable. A vista point, a turn, a sudden drop away may allow us to see something we didn't before. The path to somewhere is three dimensional, not two dimensional. Sometimes the path is safe and stable, other times it requires trailblazing, piecing together something that feels like you are ascending towards the top without a map.

Contractor, cook, competitor or commander-in-chief, there is a specific landscape that requires a specialized plan. You accumulate knowledge and execute to the best of your ability and capability. You have your toolbox, your recipe, or your game plan. Away you go, blending, and baking until you think you got it right. Maybe a mentor showed you the way to get it done perfectly. Or could it be you have no clue, need to fake it until you make it, trial and error? A conservative mindset versus a risk-taking mindset produces different energetic impressions.

To truly construct a peak performance persona, required is the ability to integrate, assimilate disparate concepts, blending them into a clarified product. For all that is important in how we think, feel, do and believe, the end product must resonate with those consuming it. When ciphering how thoughts, likes, dislikes shape mental chatter, remember to ponder the constants, their influencing properties, how their definitions add nuances to life and all that we encounter.

If there are 300 million people in various stages of evolution, being and doing, and you represent one path walker, odds you get to the top of whatever mountain you attempt to scale on the first attempt are slim. Rarely as a rookie do you get your hands on the trophy in your first attempt. It happens, but there is this thing called experience, and it's valuable.

Inherent in the debate, politics or peak performance, at any given point in time, there are only so many seats at the table, or a finite number able to attempt the summit. There isn't a whole lot of room to maneuver the higher up we climb. There are many trails we can take to get to the foot of the mountain, where yet another trail gets you to base camp. It is from the basecamp you will then attempt to summit. Thus, of primal importance is a sound plan, how you prepare yourself on the lead-up trails.

There are three parts to peaking: first, know thyself, second, respect the challenge, and third, sacred sacrifice. Duality, energy, force, geometry and balance, their construct and conditions are reminders. Five constants influencing the properties and functions of our five circles of consciousness. Talked about will be the five universal emotions on top of our five senses. But it doesn't stop there. Beyond this discussion are the five basic elements of life, (air, ether, earth, fire, and water), and what some cultures refer to as a fifth direction. The number five, all things five-pointed, is a construct discussed in detail. Everything taps into these concepts as they are universal conditions.

Don't glaze over yet. Keep the mind open to new ideas, perspectives, ways of looking at things. To know what your truth is, concepts must become a conviction. New roots must be established. The path of being and becoming is a journey, but one that takes desire to pursue. the path to self-mastery has many rewards, but like any other harvest, there is work to be done. Get rooted before you set out dropping seeds.

Serving as your facilitator to help you accomplish new feats, consider your time reading as time spent with a 'metaphysical mechanic,' a service professional well suited to perform whole-system maintenance. Relax, settle in, make yourself some tea. There are diagnostics, system checks, parts and processes that require monitoring. From this master tune-up in the works, happiness will be here soon enough.

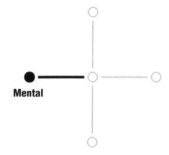

Mental

GOING MENTAL

It is no secret that our brain is an amazing entity. Billions of calculations, filtering data, categorizing audio and visual stimuli, constant neural firing managing emotions and our energy grid. Because of all that is perceived and processed, a constant stream of output is produced. Some relevant, some not.

However, for what an amazing relational database our mind represents, predicting the future from disparate points is not a forte. It can only conjure what the future might be like. The brain only knows what it has stored across thousands of files. A story always influenced by historical impressions.

An amazing hard drive with a cool user interface, functionality, and thousands of apps. Incredibly efficient capturing, pairing data, it is constantly creating new relationships and matrices, making the speed of data retrieval equally as impressive. You would imagine such a high-quality entity and processor to consistently calculate valuable and reliable data weaves. Not so much. Contemplative sects refer to it as monkey mind. Chatter, screech, jump.

The brain is the first responder in how we relate to our environment, internally and externally, consistently synthesizing an overwhelming volume of stimuli. The five senses provide endless streaming content to be translated into a personal language. So much is processed there is almost too much to say about each and every capture. Tireless input produces tireless chatter where all is not to be believed or acted upon. Filtration is important as is discernment. However, this perspective is not default-mode in our operating system. it is learned, then coded.

We know when we are happy and we definitely can summarize when we are miserable. In happy mode, the mind is behaving beautifully as pleasure dominates the senses. Nothing to overly complain about keeps us feeling good. When not in balance, not happy, a reacting mind is agitated, unsettled, seeking resolution. *I am suffering* the ego-mind says, energetic diffusion now disrupting proper rhythm and flow. Focus is lost because critical vibrant thought energy is diverted to supporting an illusion. If you think mind over matter is your practice, wait until the ego's voice joins the band.

Browse any self-help ensemble of books and be reminded of the emphasis in success is dominated by conversations addressing advanced mindsets. The broad umbrella covers multiple aspects of positive patterns in thought construction. Think this way to become that. All fine and dandy yet across a broad spectrum of personal trials, challenges, failures, and successes, there are many more support spokes that must be tightened and trued to foster high-level performance or support change.

An advanced mindset is critical to navigating our way forward or up if we are seeking a higher degree of amplitude as we torque the engine. The goal of positive patterning applied in practice requires an anything is possible belief, consistently generated, whereby the embedded energy in the intention is positive, creative.

Yet, in analyzing mind, its processes, the consciousness constant of duality reflects the mind has two sides tucked nicely under umbrellas of creative and destructive, generally positive and negative. Theoretically, we can 'practice positive' any time we desire to implement a 'feel better about ourselves' moment.

However, there are two sides to the cultivation of patterning a positive path. Positive shaping which is inherently creating, as well as a parallel practice of understanding and managing (shifting) the negative. The ultimate challenge is minimizing the constant barrage of disruptions and derailments which interrupt our rhythm and flow towards a positive energetic frequency.

The goal is to appreciate the power of positivity, applied in actions, consistently, over time. The second support, the flip side, in the practice of positive is then identifying the negative influences which produce distortion. One of the prime tenets in the law of attraction or manifestation is a sub-tenet of the Law of Free Will, consistent messaging. All seems fine and dandy, but then suddenly, one mental lapse is triggered by a barrage of negative emotions. One single day of practice fatigue and we cease, generally compromising the continuity through rationalization. Oh, I will pick up again tomorrow when I feel better.

A high percentage of the population can focus to sustain a pledge for approximately three weeks, then a lapse, something else replaces our attention grab. It's standard in the overall bell curve of attention spans in the quick grab digital era. Yet training is conditioning to be able to do more. Thus, considerations that expand beyond simple mindset training are extremely important to developing mastery of our condition on the human path.

The Magic in our Minds

Imperative as one walks a path of performance or change is the application of a positive perspective, discerning against self-limiting, deconstructing thought-forms. Game plans require assessing strengths and weaknesses, both yours and the competitors you come up against. Business plans require projections paired with execution.

Perspective, understanding we confront two sides of the mind, loops back to a constant: duality. All situations, dynamics where competition is involved, in life or sports, inherently contains a positive/creative element as well as a negative/deconstructive one. Respecting what you don't know is as important building up what you do know, what your truth is or becomes.

The proverb 'Know thyself and all will be revealed' is developing greater self-awareness through objective observation, fine-tuning, then emitting a different frequency into one's environment. Most know the warm fuzzy of a mind at ease, yet observe a mind under duress and one hears much different chatter than a mind in harmony.

Experiencing physical exertion, mental exhaustion, emotional depression depletes you, is painful, uncomfortable, and at times not sensible. But when the mind screams out in objection, commanding you stop, give up, actively debating the relevance of the torture it's enduring, an opportunity to shift your shape presents itself. This is where our brain reveals the ego mind. The 'hey big fella, can't you see my self-importance is suffering here.'

Observing, monitoring, shaping your thought process paves the path for clarity between what is intuition (positive) and what constitutes a 'head trip' (negative). Intuition is a clean feel. It is grounded energy, a comforting feel good in your gut. Generally, it is crystallized, without distortion. Head trips are confusing; ideas, thoughts jump back and forth, streaming at a speed where packets are jumbled. Head trips are unstable in their energy because they are inherently chaotic. This disposition produces a different vibration in our bodies because its position toggles. When it toggles, it is still searching for its version of truth.

In those times when life is very objective, you win or you don't, developing our intuitive mechanism becomes empowering. Calming is the energy that comes with knowing your truth, understanding, discerning purpose. The only way this calm can be experienced is by expanding the gaps of quiet between the packets of chatter. The space between thoughts it is said. Developing an intuitive channel fosters a straight-line channel for positive subconscious messages to the higher self. Isolating higher self and what comes through as messaging requires separating from the chatter, i.e. quieting the mind.

In knowing thyself we strive to discipline mental awareness towards separating valuable from clutter. Understanding how we are hardwired, what our soft programming is, what do we believe, and why? If thought forms are powerful enough to heal, they also can contain the energy to harm. Upside, the light side, is they are powerful enough to make magic, create miracles. The downside, the dense dark side, is energy which fuels our mental wheel, going around and around until we are exhausted riding it. This path literally a waste of valuable time.

Duality, energy, force, geometry, and balance. If intentions and thoughtforms are powerful forces, trumping physical force, more fully appreciated is what constitutes prayer, divine requests for assistance, or expressing gratitude, thanks for one's life. The power in sustained intention coupled with unwavering attention in executing a plan is where growth occurs. Where work is defined by consistent effort over time, the power of the mind is focused on the good, the positive, constructive, and productive. This, in turn, expands consciousness.

Judgment, hatred, intolerance are mindsets that can be set free with new information, different perspectives forcing creativity to problem solve that which is for the best and highest good of all parties involved. This is a version of sacrifice, desiring beyond the personal. Arriving at a personal truth is powerful. Doubt is debilitating. Fear can be more illusion than a real signal of danger. In oppression, we can mirror back the shame in those who oppose. Knowledge, beyond our intelligence quotient, is key.

The Two Sides of Mind

With the magic comes the muggles. Mix together all you have heard referencing the brain, the processor of mind. Left and right, like or dislike, yes or no, a maybe loiters until it can be convinced, committed to one side or the other. Conscious mind rules action whereby subconscious mind influences behavior. Learning to ride a bike is conscious; the messaging and memory around the what, how, where, when is filed away for reference. Key is what kind of message is being sent to the subconscious mind for filing. Was it a positive experience or a negative one?

For all intents and purposes, our mental processing follows a binary model. The relational database initially supports two broad possibilities, yay or nay, positive or negative. Our mind might infer something said is negative, which sets off a subsequent chain of emotional reactions. Or it strikes us as favorable data and thus we stay positive, or we are not affected. Ah, doesn't affect me you might say. A 'maybe' or 'not so sure' thought puts you on the 'no' platform waiting for something compelling to lure you back to the 'yes' side of the tracks.

If you agree that your brain can run on, seemingly out of control, it is rational to explore how to discipline, how to train our mental process. Subject to oversight, the mind is a powerful tool. However, when left undisciplined, it becomes susceptible to viruses and malware that disrupt efficiency and output.

How we interpret, react and respond to challenges, as well as how we relate to people and situations follows one of two sides, a positive inference or a negative one. Open and accepting versus judgment and resistance. Which way you go is heavily influenced by what conscious and subconscious mind come together to postulate.

The pleasant experiences, the feel-goods, joy, laughter, solving a problem, making someone smile with an act of kindness or a kind word. The inspired mind, the hungry mind identifying and crafting thought-forms which spawn productivity, spark creativity, thus right action. This mind is crafting for the highest benefit of all connected energies, energized, grounded, constructing with purpose. This is creative mind.

Conversely, there is the out of control mind. A stream that rages makes us rant. A mind that cannot stop with its commentary, opinions, and posturing. It doesn't let us fall asleep or stay present at any given moment. Angst and unsettled, it bounces back and forth, one idea to another more preposterous. You try numbing it, anesthetizing it, anything to make it stop. Blowing about in the winds of chatter, this is a fearful mind which loses traction frequently, induces panic, splinters ability to stay focused and on the path, deconstructing because it fears. The is the reactive mind.

This binary path of positive as creative and negative as deconstructive is the starting point in a new relationship with mind. In the path work of creating advanced mindsets, this is play twenty-two. First, one must observe the chatter, noting what it puts out for consideration. Did you ask for that deduction, or did it just come around by its own suspicious ego volition? This is identifying where we are in a place of creating or reacting. Are you on offense or defense?

Second, part and parcel, is positive patterning, but appreciating how first to implement positive patterning in a mind at rest versus a mind under duress. There is freedom discovered in developing the Buddhist position of detachment, how we learn to separate mental chatter from its emotional counterparts. The one key construct in developing an advanced mindset is being keenly aware that emotional disruptions are the biggest form of kryptonite to super mental powers.

It starts with shaping and applying positive perspective. What are we looking at and then, what do we want to put in? Cognitive-behavioral therapy allows us to develop a process for our intuition (truth), versus constantly ciphering a 'head trip' (non-truth).

As a practice, mindfulness is becoming more vogue. None of us when younger really dedicate time and effort to discerning what is coming out of our brain, or why. It's my brain. Why shouldn't I trust what it says? But there is too much stimulus, too much to comment on, talk about. Some of us just blather out random brain chatter. Some get perplexed, stymied, 'I will figure it out later' a commonplace expression. With time and maturity, the value gleaned from keeping an open mind becomes clear.

(At)tention. You harness mental energy and laser beam it on/at your landscape. You have thoughts, ideas and must translate those into physical doing. This is the physical attention placed on an object, goal or entity. Once the external condition is framed up, then we decide what motivation is going in. This is where we influence mind with the concept of (In)tention as a force.

There is clarified energy in the foundation of your vision. What is your spiritual motivation, what are you wanting out of your venture, your path, what is your burning desire and what is the emotional impulse driving that desire? This is the ultimate why are you wanting what you are wanting. What do you hope to get out of it? 'At' is objective; 'In' is subjective. This is clarified when we find our heart-spark.

Perspective

Is what we see what we know or what we know what we see? Life lessons and working through emotional baggage are generally not problem sets handed to us to be discussed in group settings where answers are revealed. There are no nice, neatly wrapped boxes with a packing list and a set of instructions on how to assemble a new you, or deconstruct and discard the old. If that were the case, our personal growth work would be much more straightforward.

We would have a list of that which is applicable to us and where we are in our evolution. There would be numbered steps for us to re-read, possibly frustrating the brain because there is some chatter saying this shouldn't be hard. There would be some universal index to cross-reference, a karmic GPS to make sure we are getting through the forest, on the least dangerous path with a dot showing our destination.

I am wondering these days how many people in society know their frequency of vibration. I doubt many are fully aware of soul issues or wounds established during childhood that require transformative attention. Therein lays one of the most paralyzing aspects of moving through life in that the teachings/lessons are not presented to us in a clear, crystallized form.

Unfortunately, most often our learning comes through a metaphysical portal labeled *pain and suffering, this way.* Ultimately, we are here to evolve, express love as a lasting visible marker long after we transition, not just breathe and take up space. Advanced holy men teach that humans have four levels of consciousness. We are born in at a fifth level with the potential to evolve to the eighth level, enlightenment. What clues does this offer us relative to learning and seeing things in a different light from a new perspective?

That we become aware of repetitive patterns, scenarios that play out in our lives, two, maybe three times, all leaving a familiar emotional response triggering déjà vu is mindfulness applied. When we have been defeated a third, fourth time and get the impression that something is wrong, we throw our hands up and say, wait a minute, what the hell is going on here? Is it in these moments where our lesson is wrapped in metaphor? What is it we are just not getting?

The transformational element becomes researching in rewind. Look for clues. Look for pieces of similarity in themes. Are patterns playing out? Same behavior setting you off, same scene, same shit, over and over? Different mask, but same masquerade party. What is the source of the repetitive charge in the scenarios that have been challenging? How have you acted out, reacted to an external threat? What is standardized in your behavior or your reaction that has been the same across all situations?

If you find yourself constantly posturing across situational events where there is conflict, 'this has nothing to do with me,' 'it's not my problem,' or even better, 'you just don't understand,' perspective is frozen in singularity. You can't admit to seeing things any other way, so why even consider?

Analyzing individual behavioral issues with a fresh perspective is the key to profound shifts in consciousness. One must hold space for tenets of the theory of relativity. When you shift a perspective, you see an object from a new vantage point. Fractional differences that when completed in a 360-degree roundabout might provide valuable new data points of information.

It helps to play investigator because only in analyzing how things have played out, will you get a glimpse into how one cracks the code of what the lesson is, what you need to learn from that reality. People used to tell me, "Root, you just think too much." Maybe, maybe not. I rest on my premise that metaphors abound, and if you can take some humor, some clues from the riddles, distill it down, you will see the thread that has woven all together. Man is simply a machine if we choose to not look at the interconnectedness of the overall system.

Much of the patterning we have coded is reinforced by our perspective on things. Think back to the last relationship disagreement you went through. Welling up in you is the thought that in no way shape or form were you wrong. *The other person just doesn't get me, or how do they not understand what I am talking about*, you bemoan.

Perspective, via some threads of relativity, is subjective. We see something others may not; conversely, others may have different commentary on the exact object both parties are staring down. Relational subjectivity. How you think you see things binds you in an attachment. This attachment has an emotional charge.

This is where you have to comprehend how ego operates and what needs it has to be filled, combined with any developmental wound we carry forward. If you suffer from severe emotional abandonment and are in a phase of low self-esteem, your perspective on objects, things, events or dynamics is bombarded by negative thought influences.

Plain and simple, limitation begins in the mental realm. The only way to expand out of limitation is to change your perspective. You can change your reality by changing your vantage point. The hardest exercise we as mental beings undertake is reprogramming negative thought patterns into positive expression.

I have dealt with this my whole life and have seen where trauma and old coding are tripwires that tip into engrained response patterns. It was incessant, consistently interrupting my creative and physical productivity. You think you have done the work to fix something, only to discover that you didn't get to the root of the old source code.

As we develop self-awareness into our ways of being in the world, we must re-learn there is not something wrong with others per se. Our complex formulas of mental, emotional, and energetic influences rarely are exactly like someone else's. Like DNA patterning, there are always slight variations. While all men/women are created equal, no two men/women are created exactly alike. Given that we use a fraction of our brain's processing capability, imagine how powerful feeding our heart with the right input could be.

Some perspectives align with personal or moral values. Tolerance, patience, integrity are often learned, developed in humility. Whereby, humility, in essence, holds some suffering energy, e.g.—being humbled. Holding space that opposites exist in every situation, scenario, and dynamic allows for instantaneous opportunity to be present in mindful choice.

Wherever you think you are boxed in, stuck, behind or bewitched, *stop, snap,* and *shift* your perspective. Know that if a negative emotional reaction surfaces or destabilizing thought patterns arise, make the effort to step aside from the flow of what is coming through your head, allowing space for additional information gathering, containing any negative input as best as possible.

A positive perspective is basically a ritual. Dwelling on what isn't working reinforces that energetic attraction of like kind. Turn the glass 180 degrees. Implement a mantra, a chant, something you repeat softly to yourself over and over. The mind responds well to repetitive conditioning. It is the discipline of mind focusing on possibilities, not what isn't there or isn't working.

Intention and Thoughtform

Derived from quantum physics is the postulate that there are two laws in physical systems, one of measuring and one of observing, that produces two different experiences. The relevance here is seeing intention as a force and that when that force is used to shape a vision the process of mental manifestation begins. Measuring and quantifying are comfort zones for our brain. As the mind engages in its logical/cognitive role and we are focusing on outcomes, possibilities are computed for the brain to process as a conclusion.

Vision questing: imagery work, constructing a mental image or collage is a very powerful vehicle for shaping positive mental patterns. Literally setting down the mental construct of limitation, a command is issued to dream big, think bold. There is a blank canvass where anything is possible because we imagine it as so. The freedom of believing, instituting mental programming that has a joyful, emotional charge is an accelerant. The spark of love energy that starts a small fire.

Refer to the constants introduction and retrieve the file addressing forces number four and five, imagery and spiritual intention. The transition to the next stop on the work path, our emotional circle of consciousness, encourages us at this point to 'see' things differently. Expanding beyond habits or routine to stop, snap and shift conveys to our spirit a willingness to explore, widening our lens aperture to capture a glimpse of other possibilities.

As such, in acknowledging the mind's need to quantify and rationally express, one learns how powerful it is when we reside in seeing/holding/visualizing positive pictures. If intention is a force, whatever energy is put into that image creates a distinct harmonic vibration, thus attracting or repelling respectively. Whatever energy has critical mass shapes what is manifested because of the Natural Law of Attraction. If our thinking is distorted, either by information or emotional reactions, our imagery subconsciously reflects that distortion.

Thoughtforms, not even vocalized have a high degree of esoteric force. There is no such thing as a vision without an energetic frequency. If you are so sick of a condition, at some point you just believe there is value in an alternative way of being. So exasperated, there is no other alternative. Desperation combines with hope and desire to start fresh. If you are seriously angry, spiteful, and that energy is embedded in some thoughtform, it will manifest outwardly as drama, conflict, chaos or dark comedy.

There is energy in our thoughts and our spoken word which is why creating advanced mindsets is not alone an exercise of just thinking positively. The consciousness of the mental circle creates a dual reality that highlights the teeter-totter of mind on one side and emotions on the other.

Like a horizontal board sitting atop a fulcrum, both sides must cooperate in balancing each other should we expect spectacular things to happen. Creating something starts with 'seeing' the image, layering dimensions with wishful intricacy, and then fertilizing with positive emotional energy. This is the intention injected into all things consciously built from scratch, mental and emotional sides are balanced by love.

Taking things a step farther from this micro discussion of individual balance, raising our own levels of self-awareness, turn to look out at what is being exhibited on the macro level, in culture and society. Disturbingly, negativity, bashing, and barking have become the norm. Outbursts reaffirming self-importance versus mindful expressions.

The extension is the negative energy, the bashers, that are dominating our societal conversation. Righteousness, wanting to be mad, hate someone for something is exposing where individually we appear to be failing. There is a void in today's leadership of personas standing consciously in the light, for the best and highest good of all—a concept our country was built upon, yet an attitude lost in 'what's most important to me phase' of the 'not so conscious' capitalism movement in place.

Across the board, we all must raise our game. There has been a systemic energy hack on a global scale depleting our sensibility. Deception, deceit, data hacking, the disintegration of privacy, disasters, death by A, B or C, guns, bombs, or poison. Haters wanting to hate are dominating the conversation. I don't know about you, but It's bumming me out.

Intuition versus Head-Trip

What served as one of my most valuable personal growth tenets was separating the two channels, all my head trips, mental chatter versus those places where I was able to channel what I came to know as my intuitive truth. An interesting behavioral byproduct of this work created higher self-awareness in how I responded, reacted to the words of others. And the best way to foster higher self-awareness is emotional detachment from words. When one finds that words no longer control them, only then does our perspective on how we create, change.

Over my years doing deep dives, regardless of whether that immersion was training for an impact event, or some aspect of personal growth work, hindsight around mental discipline can comfortably impart that discernment and detachment were strong lessons that required beyond average time to master. Primarily, discernment and detachment as it related to really getting into a place of trusting my intuitive voice compared to wasting vital energy spewing chatter.

Intuition is a (psychic) channel that can be developed. Like any other skill for a beginner, it requires practice, ideally under the guidance of an advanced practitioner. Intuition, knowing when truth is coming to you versus accepting a mental disposition is tricky. It takes time because it involves multiple variables. In and of itself, the art of detachment is an advanced spiritual principle. Yet in the process of quieting mind, working with our breathing cycles helps develop that place of dropping in more effectively.

What is the voice of intuition, what are head trips, and how does one know which is the real deal? Novices opening to metaphysical concepts and tenets will benefit by stating an obvious question to themselves before taking that idea deep into quiet contemplation. The answer to your query is behind the first few waves of brain chatter, chiming in to provide thought mind or ego-mind their position statement.

At a point along my path, I read where our intuitive truth is the information delivered in between the gaps of chatter. It comes strong and clear. I dare say that at some point in your life you have experienced one of those epiphany moments, a 'mini-epiphany.' Those moments when little pieces, nuggets of personal truth, pop in from nowhere identifiable. It bubbled up and in at the perfect moment, not to be doubted. It resonates with your whole system.

Looking back on the work, describing the occurrences of these a-ha moments, there is a unique sensation that arrives with the insight or flashes of information. It just drops down and in. One's internal response is almost as it understands the information is from a place of higher knowing. You don't debate it because no other system is pushing back in a counterattack.

When do you know the truth, and that what you are receiving is actually truthful? Truth is that which is absolute. In the physical realm, truth is dealt with differently than it is in the etheric realm. Intuitive truth comes to us when we open the door, seeking. It is information, or wisdom that is more macro in nature, versus micro.

An example of the intuitive red flag may be an inner voice reaffirming you should not date Mary or Joe; it could also be referred to as one of those gut feelings. Expanding on the gut feelings, later in the book, addressed is a conservation around chakras, and which chakras govern different body sections and attributes. Additional nutritional research has been sprouting addressing brain-gut correlations for body/mind health. Meta-phors abound.

When higher intelligence comes in, or when we are in conversation with our higher self, information drops in without generating an emotional reaction/distortion. It is received unequivocally, generating instant recognition of its absoluteness in your being, emotionally and mentally. It usually induces a state of humility in that the recognition of this information is honored, thus accepted immediately and not rejected by the mind. It comes in a flash when you least expect it. There is no indicator, buzzer, or flashing light that warns of its arrival. No packing slips identifying the contents. You open to it and end up saying, Yep, pretty much.

Developing an intuitive channel does not happen by gripping, tenseness, or physical discomfort in the gut. Often it is information joined by a sensation. The voice of truth is unemotional, not reactionary, yet is what you need to know at the moment. You feel it in your being. Everything in combination resonates with comfort and fosters clarity.

It may be fragments of a bigger picture or it could arrive in one big bang moment. Fundamentally, you prepare through meditative practice. If time is never taken to just be without stimulus other than the breath and breathing, the space in the gaps between mental chatter will never be discovered.

Head trip chatter is what we commonly understand as normal mind. The endless stream of commentary with a very self-centric theme. Head trip chatter comes as a stream of words when nothing has specifically been requested by the individual. It seems random, feels random and often is random. This way one day, but quite another position the day after. The streams come in waves, ebbing and flowing on the shores of Ego Island. It is reactionary;

it is a commentary with a stated position. It is posturing. *Why would I want to do that?*

It could also form as some thought conveying in superlative terms, comparative, a place of less than, greater than, or equal to the reference. That chatter is mind chatter, and sooner or later as you evolve through your refinement of being and thought, you will recognize mind chatter as it streams. It is more annoying because it is just there and takes up our attention listening to everything it spews. Up and down, back and forth.

One path to take in developing discernment is acknowledging whatever you are registering, then sitting with the information for a period of seventy-two hours without external discussion, or asking to talk outwardly about. You embrace it, don't discuss it or ask anyone for advice. This quiet process will help discern whether an emotional response mechanism has been attached. The three-day window provides patience and detachment to sit with the internal dialogue you 'heard,' reflecting on what you received. If no change in position is registered, there is no doubt what came in was your intuitive truth.

There was a Zen master who was asked, "Teacher, how do you know if a decision or voice is that of truth?"

The Master responded, "I will take the voice, decision, or message and eat it. If it upsets my stomach, gives me gas, then I know it was not right for me."

In the Huna warrior tradition, the three realms we command are lower, middle and higher self. There is a pyramid of authority. This said, engaging the higher self to establish its realm as authority needs to be a directive from the human mind.

The Huna method is to engage your higher self in the following manner. Put down in writing whatever it is that you want to receive as direction or guidance, as well as what your dilemma, choice matrix, or situation is, to be resolved. Speaking out loud, *higher self, I ask for truth recognition.* This can be accomplished by stating the paradox as best as you can. *Spirit, I am having a hard time discerning what my truth is in this matter. Help me identify, see what is for my best and highest good, that it surfaces in a manner fully recognizable to me.*

If an answer comes, sit with the insight for three days. If the truth had no emotional challenge, reaction to its arrival, this was intuitive input to be heeded. If it has changed in form, content or you actually forgot what the whole stream was about in the first place, say hello to mental chatter where ego overlay is the last guest to leave the party. Was the internal dialogue superlative in nature, positioning, judging, making one more important than the other, justifying something (e.g.—it's not my fault, it's their kind of thing)? If so, you are leaning on mental chatter.

Be open to coincidences, metaphors, things that make you smile when you see the association. Make a statement, a list, ask your questions, ask for something you will recognize (proof), read it, burn it, then wait. If it is coming from your heart, ask and you shall receive. I will admit, it is fun to see things in your outer world which appear and are precisely related to your ask.

Yes, there are going to be times which generate angst and confusion. I, too, have gone to the mountaintop praying for something that is near and dear to my heart but never received any response in general from spirit. Maybe it just wasn't in the cards. I believed, but no discernable information was received. It tested my faith momentarily. There are times when I have doubted. But then as soon as the doubt was expressed, clarity arrived in its place.

Due to the complexity of energetic variables involved, a divine standpoint, manifestation is about vibration, timing, and commitment. Any attachment out of balance with your truth, say wanting from a place of greed or power alters energy, possibly creating karma to be balanced later.

Advanced light workers have come to understand spirit doesn't give an answer as to why. It's not included in the package. You just have to have faith that for reasons not explained that wasn't the course of action, or outcome, for you as an individual to know, at least right now. This is why identifying and heeding the intuitive voice is so valuable in this work.

For those that don't pray, believe in God, or have a reference point on divinity, most likely you will negate upfront any benefit from this type of hocus-pocus talk. What is difficult for many in these types of sequences is a core message not trying to convince there is a God, merely, there is a higher self, a power outside of your conscious mind that can be engaged for rational dialogue. What a concept right?

Know your heritage, know your tribe, and know thyself. The hardest work we will do in this world while breathing will be working out our story, looking at ourselves, our past performance, our successes, our history, our pains, and our fears. There is no more difficult journey than that which takes us inward, facing our shadows, our identities, our divine heritage.

In knowing thyself, and the conscious choice to re-explore parts of your story, the process allows energy to seed new experiences, new ways of seeing and being. In developing the ability to filter truth from chatter with trust, it is as much a function of knowing what and how to ask for that which you 'see' in thoughtform and feel in your heart.

JRx

My JRx is an assessment of sorts. I will stop short of saying it's a prescription. There is no 20 mg blue pill to make sense of what is down your rabbit hole. Rather, it is a cumulative view, followed by some 'JRxercises' to foster shifts in thinking and chemistry.

Growing up as the son of a pharmacist, it was easy to learn the precision in medicinal healing. My brain took to the structure of concentrations and doses. Years spent watching customers come through the store, matching up those personas with the contents of their prescription bags was enlightening. I studied the regulars, their behavior, quirkiness, mannerisms. Slowly, with my trusted Merck manual in hand, I learned the business of pills. Better living through chemistry was the industry's mantra.

But with those years came another understanding because it brought a perspective I did not seek. Observation served up information about people that taught me things. Some of it was seeing a multitude of folks addressing concerns of mental adjustment to quell some condition, some real, some diagnosed by a duck who could quack and write prescriptions. A subtle back story watching people deal with their shit.

This experience came into play across areas of personal development work or competitive situations where I struggled with how I thought I was seeing things, people, situations. I thought I knew things, but often that thought turned out to be a falsity. I had to turn this analytical spotlight on myself, turn a 180-degree perspective, able to emotionally detach from my concept of self-importance, and see JR from a different vantage point. When I looked at my early story, I identified the rift. In the outside world, I was acting out around something that I felt on the inside.

There was a time when I was forced to completely retool my mental relationship to life and living. There was no issue in my competitive realm. Early advances in sport and competition were powered by a mental undertow of not wanting to fail versus the expectation to succeed. It produced an interesting condition, hyper-performance with a slice of 'I can make this happen' attitude because I feared being left behind.

For those officially old school, there was no learning or being taught about the power of positivity. Being addressed in a harsh tone of doing it or else didn't produce anxiety of getting sued. For me, there was just enough self-esteem-based doubt, fear and angst to serve as fuel for the fire. I was getting stuff done but it wasn't necessarily from a place of heart love, it was one big head trip getting me through each phase.

Where much of my work on performance and change happened was being forced to really evaluate my disposition, mental and verbal, with what was happening in my personal relationship realm. It took years to comprehend the tie between my emotional shortcomings and the mental dialogue chattering to support a specific feeling. Where things weren't aligning in my life showed up in relationships, personal and professional.

Headstrong, confident bordering on the cocky, opinionated, stubborn, feisty. Mix that into a bowl then stir in a little angst, anger, resentment, good looks, and charm. For many a moon, my position in relationships harbored a 'my way or the highway' addendum. I would refer to this over and over, finding myself in yet another disagreement, fight, or fuck you moment about yet something else that was seemingly my fault. At least that is how I heard things. You are a handful, what are you thinking, do you think anyone is going to put up with your shit? My response was pretty simple and consistent, "I don't need this bullshit. Later."

Years of drama, energy expended imploring my position on the world, people I said I loved. But even though I didn't think I was drama, my world seemed to reflect nothing but drama. It was a disconnect wide enough to be a rift. I tried to control others through words, intellectual rationalizations, positions, posturing, positioning, and in hindsight trying to preserve some shred of self-importance. I would always create, yet soon blow up that creation.

Break-ups were always the crazy girlfriend's fault. Leaving a job was always something my employer didn't do right or didn't see. Externalizing all results allowed me to pin it on everything else but myself. I was finally able to recognize patterns in breakups. Things that were said I could recall myself saying exactly year over year in each and almost every relationship at a stress point.

Thankfully, there was an epiphany point. Actually, it was a combination of two points. The first which took many years to identify was understanding my mind at rest was much different than my mind under duress. At rest, dealing with whatever went through my head, it was much easier to implement actual cognitive-behavioral practices around positive perspectives, how to constantly create that command.

My mind under duress proved extremely challenging to quiet, get under control so to speak. From somewhere in my brain the constant interpretation was 'I am under threat' and my 6'5" ego stepped in to make sure the real issue was being addressed. "I need you to hear this. I need to be in control. If you do this you are going to get hurt. Seriously, stop, you are right. She is stupid. She just doesn't get it."

But these interjections didn't just stay in the playground of mind. Physical sensations manifested with mental discomfort. Nausea, headaches, bloody noses, depressed, shame, embarrassment, the 'fuck I did it again' acknowledgment, nothing resembling positive. I tried to control every situation, scene or serenade with words. Shocking that my issue was that words, the emotions triggered by those words, controlled me.

I share some of these personal areas of weakness to highlight personal challenges which highlight the interplay of mind and emotions, how entanglement has to be dealt with to truly master our mental process should we hope to create a consistently positive perspective.

JRxercise

For a complex issue, there is a relatively straightforward fix. For all things thoughts, thinking and the theoretical, it is acknowledged that our primary goal in elevating performance is positive mindset. A perspective, regardless of how bleak something appears, that repeats anything is possible, over and over, is important. And because we know everything is connected, the patterning of our mind happens more quickly as we acknowledge the other half of the formula to success, monitoring, then shifting negative emotional energies.

Discerning positive energy from negative energy/influences, how each supports or interferes with consistency while patterning positive, become acts of patience strung together. Detachment is an important next level teaching after discernment, primarily because this bleeds into our emotions and overall level of emotional intelligence. Being able to stay open to new perspectives, less grounded in our ego response, helps quiet the mental chatter by restriction. Head trips become less as we consciously call upon our higher self to impart our intuitive truth.

Stop. Snap. Shift.

Positive patterning a mind at rest is best achieved by employing the spiritual Law of Substitution. A positive entity can be naturally substituted for a negative one. Because of the Law of Free Will, as humans, we can choose, but also change a choice. The Law of Free Will blends with the spiritual Law of Substitution. This highlights the power of energy with intentional creation. This is an extremely simple but powerful way to shift out of negative thoughts or expressions.

Disciplining a mind under duress I find requires implementing a container around the mental chaos. Because a mind under duress is louder, urgent, the temptation to give in to collapse and tap out so to speak is a strong inclination. This is where our tripwires set off landmines in our brain. The only way to contain is by surgical insertion. Consistent repetition of a mantra can contain the jumping mind, repetition jolting us back into rhythm and flow.

Expressed vocally, out loud (beginners) the vibration serves as a release for the physical body and energy grid. It is discipline by restraint. A mantra or chant serves best. A short sequence command which has meaning in metaphor, expressed over and over is the medicine to quell a disturbed mind.

My top five that are tried and true.

1) I am that I am.

Strength. Clarity. Conviction. Establishing new beliefs. Quelling anxiety.

This mantra reinforces the equality between man and life force. "I am" akin to the divine intelligence. Repeat one hundred times.

2) I am a being of violet fire, I am the purity that God desires.

Purification. Balance. Healing. Soothing. Cooling (a mind on fire)

This, the prayer of St. Germain, serves best to purify the mind, body of negativity. Violet (amethyst) is the sacred color of enlightenment. While chakras are discussed in the energetic section, the area of entry for this imaginary light is through our pineal gland (mid-forehead). If you are familiar with Kundalini work, moving energy consciously up and down our chakra grid, the violet light settles into our body from up high, descending into our physical system.

This chant should be done at first thirty-three times in succession. Advanced practice calls for three groupings of the application, morning midday and prior to sleep.

3) Everything is good and beautiful.

Steer a mind away from distortion, dissonance. Conviction. Everything has a positive position in your life. Reinforces natural law. I am always free to decide what is for the best and highest good in any moment. The accelerant for this mantra is repetition with a large smile on your face.

Repeat until you can feel the shift from frowny face to a fresh face.

4) I let go to let God (For agnostics: I let go to let good grow)

Good when feeling desperate, down or depressed. Offloading pressure. The acknowledgment that you want your higher self to lead the train. Humbleness. Humility.

Strong chant for releasing or relinquishing something. Mentally imagine what you want to let go neatly wrapped in boxes, sealed containers. These are not being discarded, merely given back to the universe for repurposing.

88 times.

5) Wamma Chi (Slow and methodical pace)

Native American divination for the Great spirit. Restoring order. Organizing mind. Inviting creation. Good for quiet under the breath mantra while in action, walking, working. This mantra squashes mental discord.

One hundred times. (Two zeros are pieces of infinity, where everything is connected. All being one).

All of these practices foster shape shifting. Mental shape-shifting is agreeing to 'C' things differently. Take any challenge, competition, conflict or conundrum, and adopt the perspective to shift what you can control, the choice in how you relate to any situation. A consistent positive perspective is learned behavior. We all have our programming, stored files from long ago. If these files contain material which was labeled as negative, the code we write for our apps is influenced by the material in that file. Our perceived strengths and our unspoken weaknesses flavor how the mind cooks ingredients offered up by the five senses. External stimuli are gathered, quickly separated into two bowls: pleasure/pain, love/fear, can/can't, will/won't, like/dislike.

The primary ingredient in Manifesting 101 is believing anything is possible. For that to be a reality, deep in subconscious files, a kernel of core belief supporting that idea needs to be stored. If something is interpreted as contrary to a core belief we hold about what will benefit us, each circle of consciousness has a reaction. There is harmonic distortion. If our perspective refines information into a negative packet, sends that packet to the subconsciousness, it is a file with a negative charge.

Constructing positive core beliefs, e.g.—positive subconscious messaging, about what we are, can do, and are willing to do, is a consistent practice of creating versus reacting. For it to take root as a daily practice, it is necessary to acknowledge the two sides of the mind, the positive, and the negative, along with the accelerants of emotions and how emotions can support or derail mind.

Our mind is a system heavily influenced by the emotional realm. A similar grouping perspective will be stated later in the material as physical body and energetic grid relationship is addressed. This is relevant as we look at all variations of energy, including emotional energies that support or distract productivity and performance.

Mental   Emotional

FEELING EMOTIONAL

Nary a day goes by without dodging, dealing, discerning and doing. Happy produces a light sensation. Movement feels easier; there is a feeling of flow in your step. Things appear to be going smoothly. Conversely, a bad day, a dull day, or an intense day, whatever the perceived emotional weight, there is a density to our demeanor, a burden, a heaviness. The good days, bad days conversation up for processing umpteen thousands of times.

The add-on to all things mind, thinking and thought creation, is the palette of emotions. If emotional energy were different colors, the metaphor is shade and hue, coloring how we see things as well as how we are seen. They stand alone or can be mixed creating new tints. Bold or bland, our emotions hold potent energy which ultimately can help, or hinder, any given performance.

Personal growth work focused on evolving beyond limiting patterns relies heavily on emotional intelligence. The term, EQ, emotional quotient, is referenced when talking EI, but where-as IQ can be quantitatively measured, EQ is more obtuse. The more emotionally aware, theoretically the higher one's

EQ. Understanding the different layers of emotions, how they influence thought construction and mental perspective is of equal importance. How we relate to feelings is a learned choice, creative or reactive.

Increasing our emotional intelligence becomes a high priority as we look for different ways of being, coping, creating. The work centers around being able to identify a core emotion, then determine how to manage (or leverage) the corresponding energy embedded. If the energy is debilitating, the practice expands on the stop, snap, shift mental exercise. Observing, containing, and channeling is the mastery turning reactive behavior into that of creative action. Understanding our basic feelings, how they affect our mental and physical body, raises emotional intelligence.

Decades ago, Peter Salovey and Jack Mayer presented the concept of emotional intelligence as the ability to: 1) perceive emotion; 2) integrate emotion to facilitate thought; 3) understand emotions; and 4) regulate emotions to promote personal growth. This mission statement encompasses four primary emotional actions which addressed viewing emotions as useful sources of information that help one to make sense of and navigate the social environment.

Salovey and Mayer postulated that by perceiving, using, understanding, and managing emotions, individuals were then able to leverage this intelligence to achieve wider cognition, better equipped to respond to our environment.

Adding to the precepts of Salovey and Mayer's ability-based model, Daniel Goleman proposed an emotional competencies model. This model focuses on emotional intelligence as a wide array of competencies and skills that drive leadership performance. Through self-awareness, self-management, social awareness, and relationship management, we are better equipped mentally, emotionally, and physically to perform at a higher level, translating into performance success.

Most valuable in their findings and research addressing emotional responses is the need to be vigilant in *relationship* management. Not just personal relationships, e.g.—husband, wife, children, girlfriend, boyfriend, but in understanding that we are all in relationship with something, every moment of our waking life. Harking back to Einstein's Theory of General Relativity, we are always viewing objects with a perspective, and from this dynamic create a relationship with said object.

Emotional intelligence per Wikipedia encompasses four capabilities:

1. The capability of individuals to recognize their own, and other people's emotions.
2. Discriminate between different feelings, label them appropriately.
3. To use emotional information to guide thinking and behavior.
4. Manage, and or, adjust to adapt environments or achieve goals.

Solving major challenges or envisioning a new reality is a quest. 'What do I really want in my life,' bases down to a clear vision, a thought construct colored by a feeling. Dreaming big, envisioning something you want, trying to solve something in your mind you don't see in the moment, there is ample positive emotional energy (hope and belief). We don't dream big feeling angry, sad, worried or fearful. Dreaming big is accompanied by joy, happiness without constraints. See, smile, feel, do.

How we set and accomplish goals, how we increase capacity for mindful communication, how we create in partnership is fueled by emotional energy. Goal-setting becomes a vision quest of sorts. Where clarified thoughts merge with a discerned emotional energy, the pitter-patter of heart energy begins thumping. This is why imagery and visualization exercises are so powerful. Conscious action promoting a supercharged subconscious message.

Constructing a vision in the mind crystallizes a desire. Akin to a basic chemistry experiment. Fill a beaker with positive thoughts, thoughtforms, then pour in the octane of creative desire. The blend bubbles up and over in reaction. Emotional intelligence helps us sift through all possibilities of 'being and becoming' so we align and balance positive thoughts with positive emotional energy.

Through self-awareness, self-management, social awareness, and relationship management we are better equipped mentally, emotionally and physically to perform at a higher level, achieve performance success if you will. Developing a higher emotional quotient advances our understanding as to why we make the choices we do, helping to objectively evaluate whether an emotion is serving us in a positive or negative manner.

You would make a perfect physician. I think you would do great as a painter. You are so talented, why don't you go into sales? Maybe you should think about getting a job so you can pay your bills, and get out of the house? Don't you want to get married, have a family? Why are you sitting around all day smoking pot, playing video games with your friends?

Outside opinions will always be there to chime in. But at the end of every day, what do you want and how do you make it happen? Doesn't seem like such a tough proposition, right? But if we get way far down a road and wake up one day muttering, "what the *%#* am I doing?", well then, it is time to get out the sketch pad and begin doodling.

Sometimes we make conscious sacrifices, compromises to hold a safe path. Other times we are living our dream and love what we do. It's the 'tweener' zone that keeps us postulating on the mother of all Achilles heels, the quicksand of 'what if.'

The Five Universal Emotions

Emotions act like the weather; they gust up, blow on through, causing enough of a disturbance to get us to briefly focused on what we feel, what is coming up. The paradox to be solved becomes when and why we attach to an emotion, a condition, then dwell longer and deeper than necessary. We know weather passes eventually, so don't obsess when it's rainy and cold. Dwelling (restriction) compromises bandwidth.

Emotions are interpretations of complex states made up of many chemical and hormone interactions creating changes in our nervous system, which in turn creates internal or external movement. The basis of the word emotion is "to move." An injection of adrenaline, for instance, increases heart rate and blood pressure. Emotional states *indirectly* affect behavior. They do not cause it. When we are feeling angry, we are more likely to act aggressively. When we are relaxed, we will more likely take time to make decisions.

If you grab something to draw on, create four circles in a north, south, east, west point orientation. In the center of those four circles, another will be placed center diamond. Anger, fear, worry, sadness/grief, and joy can be viewed as five big buckets. For me, objectifying emotions by listing in a two-dimensional setting helped objectify their illusions. Offshoot emotions, resentment, righteousness, bitterness, shame, guilt, inadequacy, find their place in one of the aforementioned buckets.

A quick glance confirms a solemn fact. Say you placed a circle at the north node and labeled that bucket anger. Fear out the left, worry the other side of the teeter-totter on the right. The south circle becomes sadness/grief. Evenly spaced are four primary emotions in a north, south, east, west configuration.

With our fifth emotion, joy, label that bucket smack dab center. What you notice are four emotions that are, in essence, negative energy which require monitoring, to be managed, minimized, or shifted. Four buckets of perceived suffering surrounding the only positive energy bucket, that of joy/happiness.

Of the five primary universal emotions, joy is a base emotion we consciously create. Yes, joy can just happen to us, but for the most part, especially as we progress in age, we come to appreciate joy as something like an ongoing art project. It is a therapeutic practice to cultivate daily, painting the picture we want.

If four of our five primary emotional buckets are conditions that require energy to observe, manage, process and discern, this takes up mental time and requires an allocation of energy to support said reactions. Depending on what emotional wounds we carry, negative emotions consume bandwidth, allocating our focus and attention to a temporary fire drill.

We don't intentionally wake up to set our intention as having a day filled with anger, fear, worry or sadness. It's not logical when we are sentient beings that have free will, freedom to choose anytime we decide. The rational mind doesn't compute that our day will go better if we are sadder than everyone else.

Doesn't really seem fair to have eighty-percent of our emotional construct stuck in reactive mode. Kind of a bleak reality, don't you think? Maybe this is why Buddhists put forth the postulate, life is suffering; four emotions we 'deal with' versus only one we intentionally create.

Anger is rarely used creatively and almost always manifests destructively. Anger is aligned with fire. Fire as we know can burn things or be used as light, heat or as a necessary force to generate energy. A person in a chronic state of anger cannot think clearly. Body areas affected by ongoing anger are the liver, gallbladder, and immune system.

Fear, or chronic bouts of fear, is a perpetual negative reaction to the reality around us. It can also be primal, unconscious. Generally generated when we are overwhelmed, unable to cope, not able to think ourselves away from a situation which we intuit as dangerous, harmful, or unstable. Ongoing fear contributes to low self-confidence which materializes in the behavior of keeping up a front for the world to see. Physical areas affected by persistent fear are kidney, bladder, renal organs, central nervous system, and endocrine glands.

Anxiety/Worry instigates energetic spikes that keep us in a heightened state of relative chaos. The opposite of calm. Persistent anxiety is acidic to our system. It impedes our ability to consistently generate positive thought patterns, worried that something is going to fail us, thus constantly raining on our parade. Physical areas that are depleted by ongoing angst include stomach, spleen, and pancreas. Our inability to digest becomes literal and figurative, possibly creating blood sugar issues, system crashes.

Grief/Sadness sucks the wind out of our sails, weakens our spirit and slows digestion. This can induce lethargy, reclusiveness, impeding appetite, a precursor to depression. Prolonged sadness sucks the water, the moisture out of our life. Body parts affected are those moist and sensitive, lungs and large intestine. Grieving the loss of a loved person, a loved pet, or a loved wish that didn't happen, isn't something that can shift overnight. It must be respected, but also managed after the initial phase of grieving 'love' lost.

Joy is amplified happiness. It moves us, lifts our spirits, warms our mind and body. Joy causes an energetic uptick because it is experienced in our heart-center, the true engine of our machine. As much as this is the one positive emotion we discover and experience, joy is light, not dense, and the single emotion that heart-sparks creative expression. The heat in joy resonates with the heart, circulatory system, and small intestine.

Is Believing Seeing?

Statistics and patterns can predict; they are markers by which we rationalize cognitive decisions. If you watch sports competition video, isolate individual tendencies, you learn a lot about how to defend, how to attack, how to contain. You develop methods, schemes, and reactions based on the probability of something happening. Whether war, sports, relationships, getting promoted, the realm of offensive and defensive schemes, our faith mechanism feels most sound when seeing is believing. We want proof.

Common is the need to see to believe. When doubt is so vehemently embedded as a belief, *prove it to me* becomes our first response. If we are to be successfully crystallizing a vision for that which we want to become, manifest, do, faith is bolstered as a byproduct of trust. The paradox here is that trust is earned. Faith is not an entity to be quantified.

Faith is a very individual disposition; however, faith is strengthened by experience. Faith is something that is built up over time, yet can also be destroyed in a fraction of that time. An existential crisis is on some level losing faith. Ironically, exactly what faith is predicated upon, believing, is where believing becomes seeing.

Becoming a believer involves many occasions of asking the universe for a sign. *Show me something God because I have lost my way; Spirit, manifest something so I will know my prayers have been heard.* It might not be quite this dramatic, but these calls to the divine we have all made. When in a place of despair, we defer to a source we think is outside of us, more powerful than us, and we hope, most compassionate towards our relative helplessness in the moment. But is it not to placate our minds that we ask/ need to see proof?

The paradox is frequently we are told to believe this or that. Innately, we come into the world trusting. Yet by the time we are adults, we seemed to have been burned over and over, blaming our naiveté for a problem at hand. Nice people get taken advantage of. Assholes leave a trail of rank bitterness. Our innocence long ago burned by the dragon in others. How does one break this cycle to embrace and embody this elusive thing termed faith?

It is very easy for us to believe, to have faith when we are continually fed examples or proof as it were, of that which we have asked for in our thoughts, in our prayers, on our daily wishlist, or even from others. But there are times in all cycles of life whereby we are challenged, sometimes for years on end. It is in those days, months, and years when we think we can't take another blow to the body, heart, or ego. As you check in to ascertain what degree of faith you have developed in your life path, ask the following, "is seeing believing, or believing seeing?"

Remember, we attract or draw into us, that which brings us closer to our personal truth. Some refer to this as Dharma or karma. These energetic attractions are often emotionally (charged) and can take the form of lessons we each need to learn. Understanding why you keep attracting the same type of distrustful person can be a clue that you do not trust yourself on some level. How can this be and why is a discussion only you will discover. Observing ourselves in emotional response, we get better envisioning what we really do want, in part because when we cipher negativity, it is clearer what we don't want. This is a powerful recognition.

We can begin to quiet extraneous mental chatter as we set healthier emotional foundations. Going inside, sitting with the mind, quieting through breath and observed breathing, we align mind and hara. In the gut (from the solar plexus down) we confront the emotional energies related to tenseness, constriction, lack of flow. It also blends themes of honor and shame.

It is here in our bellies where we resonate with, thus give energy to, the visions we have mentally crafted. "Feel it in your gut." When we believe our own vision, put consistent intention behind that which we do believe, we begin to see things coming together, without the emotional commentary coursing through our physical story. The moment you know, without emotional interference, that you feel your personal truth is the moment of epiphany.

Emotional Vision Questing

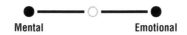

Mental   **Emotional**

Vision questing in native traditions involves sacrifice, faith, and the willingness to let go of all tethers to sustenance, mental, emotional and physical. Beyond the mental and physical challenge of going without food, water, shelter for days, vision questing is essentially where we find our emotional energies activate and we are forced to face our shit. Separation from material needs is listening to the ego-mind complain incessantly about what isn't for its best and highest good. *This foolishness must stop immediately*, it chatters.

It is in this process whereby we confront but also create. Through surrender and acceptance what becomes isolated is the knowledge of how much power lies in the emotional realm. Beyond thought, and before we examine the underpinnings of physical and energetic circles of consciousness, one learns how constructive, or destructive, emotional expression can be.

In Vision questing we confront fear, illusion, anxiety, instability and the host of nefarious energies which surface as a last line of defense the ego emanates to defend its position of importance. It is also where we can focus energy through the heart-center to balance the chatter.

Chances are whatever the difficulty, most likely you are not going to die. In desperation or crystalized desire, we create a laser beam of resilience powered from hope in the heart that we want something to change or happen differently. It is where we strip out of the normal and find the atypical, in whatever form that takes for us.

JRx

Training towards a permanent state of positivity is in part accepting how emotional disturbances storm our estate, so to speak. Part and parcel to mental training is understanding we have to be in balance. Yet, we are emotional beings living in a denser world which creates systemic stress. Continually we are bombarded with emotional energy bound up in thoughts, perspectives, beliefs and outside actions or events.

In the quest to stop, snap, and shift our perspective we learn to see things differently. The practice expands into the emotional circle, truly 'C' things differently by shifting what we can control.

Bring forward some of the tools discussed. Duality shows us we have a dual realm choice matrix. We accept, subconsciously concede, but try to convince our system otherwise. Conversely, the challenge is acknowledged, respected. Turning to our ability to exercise free will we can actively identify what we can control. Leveraging the spiritual law of substitution, you don't need to respond in anger. Fear is an illusion that you recognize creates drama. Worry is a siphon that constantly keeps us checking our devices. Sadness/grief often feels like our heart has gone through waterboarding, suffocating, weighing on our chest.

Reminding ourselves we have superpowers; the following exercise keeps us in a positive perspective. Find a blank sheet of paper and turn it sideways so it's a long rectangle. On the top half, in spaced block letters, write:

REACTIVE

On the left side margin, list anything you can think of that defines a challenge, conflict, competition, choice or conundrum. Here we are beginning to tag and release emotional observations back into our wild. Seeing things differently is aided by staring right at the large 'C' in the middle of reactive. Now, stepping into your imaginarium, use that large 'C' as a container for all the elements you wish to 'C' differently. If the goal is to shift what we can control, many of our negative influences can be housed under a 'c' word.

In your imaginarium, reflect on the list of 'c's, delving a little deeper into observing a feeling or thought that surfaced when writing it down. Can you begin to identify behavior or thoughts that were solely reactive in nature? *Oh, I don't like that person, what they said doesn't matter.*

Was there a quiet 'oh, shit' or pit in your stomach while pondering one of your C listings. Unsure, insecure, nervous or excited? Was a choice made proactively or out of a response to quell an issue, solve a problem, change the way you feel, or to change someone's disposition? Here you are trying to identify where reactive and negative align.

With the 'C' container filled by your little 'c' list, now it is time to see things differently. We can literally shift and re-create. Isolating the 'C' in reactive, we literally shift what we can control. Cut and paste that C, moving to the front of reactive. A simple maneuver with seriously powerful implications. In one move, you shift from:

R E A 'C' T I V E

To

'C' R E A T I V E

You have just harvested power. This is literally shifting what you can control. Moving what you can, changes the energetic force in the action. Here we have shaped a new perspective, (simply) creating opposed to reacting. No longer are precious resources siphoned, stolen, by the nefarious negative. In one fell swoop, you went from being down a score to a last-second Hail Mary that was never in doubt. In your deepest despair, you prove anything is possible with one deft chess move.

Now review your list of challenges, conflicts, competitions, or choices, and begin to determine how you can be creative in your problem-solving. Over time you will appreciate how much energy and time is dedicated to us reacting to negative stimulus. Once we can begin to shift out of reacting, towards creating, a major mental perspective shift has begun. You begin to notice you feel more grounded, more at peace, less sensitive, less volatile. You can sit back, watch the weather with wonder, appreciating instead of complaining.

This parallels creative and reactive discussed earlier and ties together the mental and emotional realms. It becomes an exercise in self-awareness and in some ways cognitive behavioral therapy. Anger, we know by experience, is disruptive, yet we can also learn how to channel its energy.

Fear we come to understand as illusion, keeping us from doing something that may, or may not serve us. Sitting down to have imaginary tea with your fearful foe isn't that scary. Talk over tea. Addressing fear allows the energetic impact to dissipate. Energy that can be shifted from restrictive to expansive, allowing for more relief, joy, happiness.

Worry we appreciate as the slow-burning acid it is. Anxiety, often rooted in control or self-esteem issues keeps our attention in OCD mode. Is everything going to be alright our default definition? Letting go, shifting perspectives, taking ownership of what effect we have in dynamics promotes mental clarity with emotional safety.

Sadness and grief the desolate road we travel as we learn how to come back to love and joy. It is learning to be ok with being alone. It is asking our heart to stay open and not close due to emotional pain.

Getting stuck in negative reactions or patterns saps our attention and vital energy stores. As our EQ rises, gained is the ability to stay more on the positive side of duality opposed to its opposite dark kernel of matter. Practicing detachment and discernment allows placing some space between cause and effect. Understanding how fast we negatively respond even if not stated out loud saves us time, energy, and the need to recover. Clean power is found from mindfully mining the good from the not so good. A positive expression, believing becomes seeing.

Not all emotional responses have to shock our nervous system into a panic alert mode. Raising emotional intelligence corresponds to an ability to also craft positive use for so-called disruptive/negative feelings. The advanced work towards a peak performance requires stretching beyond self-perceived limitations, identifying where energies can be harnessed and utilized as fuel.

Highlighted in CBT is an applied dynamic whereby intentional use of negative energy can be termed 'productive' worry or anger. High achievers, thinkers and grinders, OCD'ers to some degree fuel their drive applying nervous energy. Anger can be synthesized into motivation, minus resentment.

Experiencing fear where that fear isn't triggering a quantifiable threat to your survival, can be shifted through creating backup plans, countermeasures. Or you can also set aside an imaginary playdate to sit down, meeting your fear, asking what all the fuss is about.

Fear of failure, for example, would require differentiating between an emotional wound and cognitive knowledge no harm will occur by stepping into a situation when properly prepared. Grief and sadness don't have to become depressingly paralyzing. Opportunities to shift into deeper spiritual perspectives involve gratitude, selfless service, getting out of your own mind's spiral by giving without expectations.

These acts assist in shaping 'silver lining' thinking. Acknowledging what is and what isn't without emotional attachments or ego posturing. For all intents and purposes, the shift represents a conscious redirect from darker/denser to lighter/brighter.

Alas, we have joy, happiness. The one shining light which melds passion and perspective into purpose. Our happiness seems to ebb and flow as a state of being. Life is hard, seemingly harder as we grow older, set in older ways. Experiencing happiness is a welcome state of feeling, yet highlights the sensation in a cause and effect manner, e.g.—something made me happy.

JRxercise

Conducting an emotional check-in, keeping principles of the mental realm handy, can be a straightforward way to minimize debilitating emotional rushes, begin leveraging towards positive patterning, shifting what we can control.

Bring forward to memory the following goals of shaping mind.

- The stated goal is that of developing advanced mindsets.

- Primary intentional energy is to minimize the negative chatter, create and channel the positive. Highlighted perspective is reactive to creative.

- 'C'ing things differently fosters a shift in perspective, self-observing, shifting what we can control.

- Stop. Snap. Shift.

- Monkey mind can be disciplined by applying the spiritual Law of Substitution. As creator of your thoughtforms, you can replace what you don't want with something you do want. Extract the negative; insert a positive.

- For the mind under duress, including extreme emotional duress, best to employ a mantra, chant, song, something short, strong. Controlling mental duress, (freakouts, panic attacks, distress, etc.) is best accomplished by repetition and structure for the brain.

With these behavior tools, now overlay a simple exercise involving pen and paper. Pretend the aforementioned 'tools' are listed neatly in your left margin. Make a vertical list left of center on the page of each emotional bucket:

> Anger
> Fear
> Worry
> Grief/Sadness
> Joy

Isolate and contemplate each emotion as it relates to your being, what you feel is most exhibited in your overall behavior, then number from one to five, one representing most prevalent, five the least present. Remember, these represent broad umbrellas of emotional coverage. If you were to say resentment or bitterness was your challenge, would you put it under anger or fear? If you are a depressive, grief/sadness might be your number 1. Addiction issues most often fall under control which we embed under the fear umbrella. (When in doubt refer to Freud's work).

Next, utilizing the same list, now with your numbers assigned, go opposite to the right side of the page and list two states of feeling that you consider the opposite state of being. For instance, anger's opposite look to you could be calm, grounded, or peaceful. Fear's opposite to you might be courage, mindfulness, or control. For joy, it might be something like misery, resentment, disease. It becomes a personal association, but you get the idea.

Immediately, what pops from the association process is acknowledging we rarely seek to shift out of joy. Especially true if the opposite state of being lists death, misery, disease, or something dark and dense. This starts as our wake-up call. Once we get to joy/happiness, you don't consciously try to leave.

For the other four primarily negative emotional states, we flip the script by applying the mental realm tips and tools. Each emotional state will be the focus for one entire day. The goal is to monitor the emotion's appearance in your being, become aware of its energy, then stop, snap and shift.

If working with anger on a particular day, and your opposite association is calm, peaceful, Zen, when you feel anger coming in, develop a tapping habit, tap, tap, tap on a surface or on your body. This will become the subconscious signal to stop, snap, shift. Interject the command to shift perspectives by telling yourself something grounding, guiding you towards the opposite state of being from the emotion you are working on. To make the transition smooth, remind yourself to center and focus on five slow in and out-breath cycles, from your gut, not your chest.

Example in practice: I am on the phone at work, not getting the news I was relying on to wrap a project. Someone didn't do their job right, and I am pissed. The more I try to debate, the more inflamed I become because it is obviously someone else's fault and fuck up. Damn. It washes into my being. I feel it, but quickly realize that is not the energy I want to expand into, so I tap, tap, tap on my thigh. In the moment, I stop, say out loud to myself:

Stop. (I don't want to be this way)

Snap. (I see a different way of being)

Shift. (Breathing, I gather my wits, let go of my judgment, shift into problem-solving mode)

Then begin your mantra. As you go about your immediate activities, keep repetition as the new structure the brain is to follow. Let the anger energy blow on by like the weather. Whether anger, fear, worry, or sadness, the process remains the same.

When it comes to our bucket of joy, if you are in your bucket of joy, splashing around, smiling, giggling, by all means, take the rest of the day off. If you are striving to find joy, close your eyes, drop into a hard smile, and know that happiness grows when watered. Approach it as a daily art project. Do something small to make yourself happy and build out your vision. Be content, with gratitude, sitting quietly and smiling about that.

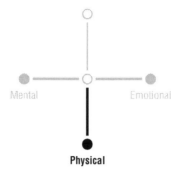

Mental
Emotional
Physical

GETTING PHYSICAL

Balance in Motion

I f you are already mentally fatigued from balancing the mental/ emotional teeter-totter, hang on, because this is where things get physical. Actualizing all that is thought and felt, attention is now placed firmly on all things doing. When an objective has been set in conceptual motion, a rough game plan must be constructed because there are quantitative markers to check. It is revisiting the 'know thyself' proverb. Quantifying your physical strengths and weaknesses as you realistically set performance goals.

Regular physical activity, e.g.—working out, is not an ingrained habit for many. But there are a plethora of benefits in the byproducts of physical exertion. The concept of oxygenating the brain stimulates a multitude of endorphins (nature's feel-good chemical) inducing brain waves which promote 'being in the flow' of things. Breath and breathing, muscle endurance, good reflexes, proper blood pressure are the most obvious benefits.

The indirect benefit of physical activity building towards the strenuous surrounds the metaphor of heart, all the heart as a muscle represents. Having spent years training and competing was a very front-line experience drawing into the proverbs heart represents. Ironically, finding my heart-center in non-sport professional endeavors seemed more elusive.

As much as it is our literal pump, the muscle of our physical machine, there is a vast reserve of energetic potential that comes along with activating our heart-center physically and philosophically. The physical center of life support, it also is our cauldron for creating joy. It literally becomes the heart-spark in grand performance.

When we perform, do or accomplish something to a higher degree than we have previously, there is transformation, subtle and great. Climbing the proverbial ladder in anything requires a combination of forces applied in unison towards a focal point. We harness vital energy to crystallize ideas, hone thoughts, answering questions in our minds enabling us to think something through. From mental and emotional processes, we arrive at the third of four foundational pillars, the physical body, and its mechanisms. Here, it is all about balance in motion.

The balance is appreciating what we generate, but also what we are consuming. Being aware of what we consume for the body (and mind) requires looking at our feedstocks, organic and inorganic, tangible and intangible. Incorporating the horizontal interplay, how mind and emotions push/pull, back and forth, we now incorporate the vertical axis of elements, our physical body system, and energetic grid.

In this realm of consciousness, the proverbial physical is all about a game plan. The what, why, when, where, and how all get answered as we look towards peak performance. All game plans require two-directional analyses: think forward, but prepared to reverse engineer your construct, your plan. Conviction and flexibility are of paramount importance.

Drawing a schematic from an engineering standpoint is fundamental. A game plan arises as a result of observation, planning, strategy, and operations, translating that into words, a picture or map. Reverse engineering is confirming that the output and the input are balanced. Approach this phase as taking yourself into a mechanic for a physical tune-up.

Unique to everyone in the competitive universe is a skill set or ability that is beyond average. For some athletes, you can see at a young age there is just something special going on; he or she was just wired for whatever they are doing. However, while everyone can dream and desire the same objective, dual realities show there is going to be someone better, stronger, faster, guaranteed. There is the podium, then the rest of the pack. There is a game plan for getting to the next level and rough game plan for just staying competitive.

Game plans can become very intricate. It is much more than a 'go forth and conquer' attitude. Accumulating a multitude of facts and reference points, factoring out projections is akin to a business plan for a start-up. You can have all the brains, good looks and feel good huggers on your team, but if you have miscalculated your competitive set, a new obstacle has been created. Thus, learn from your mistakes and recover quickly. Reverse engineer from losses, adjust, reassess. Rare is the straight line to a trophy.

Know thyself involves taking inventory, understanding what raw materials exist, being objective around what doesn't exist, or hasn't yet been discovered. It requires confidence and a healthy dash of moxey confronting obstacles to move up the ladder. Can you hit a time, make quotas, strike with precision, negotiate skillfully, create value with your participation, or manage stressful situations more deftly than the team handling the crisis? Can you outthink, out hustle, out love your competition? All questions one must be ready to face and truthfully answer.

Fundamentally Speaking

There is only so much room at the power table. Whether politics, business, sports, or cause, often a few make decisions for many. Across our lifetime, we will spend endless hours working hard towards a goal that may, or may not, ever be recognized. This is the toil of the human condition. The hard work cannot be substituted. Nothing gets accomplished by wishing and hoping. The first part of any performance path is mentally gearing up.

Training towards totality is the least glamorous part of success, including skill mastery. While there are many mini-games in life, remember the real game isn't over until you die. Mentally showing up sets in motion waves of positive energy.

Every life dynamic we encounter has patterns, moves, counter moves, techniques that involve force, energy, structure, and geometry. Footwork, balance in motion, is paramount for many sports. Prospecting, managing, selling, closing, reporting, striving to advance are essential in business and building experience. While there is a bigger macro picture, mastering fundamentals is all about tending to the micro, the precision.

Appreciate that a cake will never get icing unless the basics required to bake a good cake have been mixed in proper proportions. Dense, not dense enough, bland or too salty, recipes are intentionally precise. The same goes for anything we want to cook up in life. Master the fundamentals, especially if you are a young adult wanting to compete at a higher level. If you somehow or someway bullshit your way into a position, sports or life, you will be exposed. if you can't walk your talk, smack comes back with a whack.

There is no easy way of getting better at something. Mental lapses, emotionally self-destructing, physically cramping up can all be experienced when the entire body is under duress. There are a multitude of systems in play for us to be in top form. What we eat and drink is as important to what we consume energetically through our five senses. Absorbing drama, shocking news, abusive words, and threatening behavior are as important to manage against as the nutritional value of our feedstocks, what we put into our system for energy and sustenance.

Beyond what we eat, drink and absorb, also at our disposal is the power of how we energize, support our physical body in peak performance through consistent, positive life force we generate each and every day. Our breath, tapping into the cadence of breathing, both at rest and while under stress or duress is super important. Calculated breaths can calm, stabilize a frenzied mind. Activated breath, yelling, singing, preaching, teaching, screeching amplifies our frequency.

Pleasure and Pain

Yes, training can be a pain, but so can be going into the office every day for forty-five years. Some deal with structure better than dealing with pain. Mental, emotional, or physical, pain and pain management are the largest health care costs in America because they are the most debilitating energetic condition to endure and be productive. Being in pain is very draining.

Growing up in the world of pharmacy and pharmacology during the '80s was an eye-opening experience. What you learn is big business pretty much has something you can take to alleviate physical and emotional pain. There are more legal ways to escape than ever these days. However, now with the increase in opioid addiction, hardcore substances have worked their way onto the challenge list.

The daily list of minor physical annoyances combined with mental or emotional angst can quickly push us towards something to make it go away. The obvious distraction in our choice matrix, do I want to experience pleasure or deal with the pain. The instant gratification society we are trends to guide us towards the quickest fix.

I like to state there are different kinds of pain; Reminder pain and Portal pain. Reminder pain, predominantly body-based, is something you should be careful trying to push through. Healing broken bones, repairing soft tissue, ligaments, tendons, any physical limitation uses pain as a signaling system. Ouch, still sore and still hurts guides our decision making.

Portal pain, i.e.—emotional pain, is a separate mechanism and is tied tightly to energetic systems and neural responses. Emotional pain affects the physical, mental, energetic, but most importantly the heart-center. Emotional wounds, traumas, breakups, death, disease, even shaming, bullying and sexual harassment. Factoring emotional pain is more elusive, but it is a different pain because it highlights there is something that still needs healing.

Blowing out a knee is painful but so is losing a loved one. Pain serves as a reminder, but it can also be a portal to a wider universe of understanding. Along these lines, Stanford Neuroscience along with other research departments announced they had identified two separate locations in the brain which register physical and emotional pain. This is extremely significant as it relates to systems of consciousness. The research identified two different locales responsible for how we process recognition and mental responses.

In sports and training, there is a healthy amount of positive pain. Conditioning promotes expansion which means boundaries are getting stretched, things are getting worked, worked out, conditioned to do something better. Pushing into new ways of doing presents psychological and physical opportunities for triumph. Getting to the next level, taking the next ascent up the mountain is highly satisfying.

Proving to yourself something can get done, proud and satisfied of the work put in, temporary pain morphs into temporary pleasure. This would be an example of physical portal pain. Having voluntarily moved through a difficult phase, a reward is presented; the reward manifests as pride or that endorphin 'high' after exertion and execution.

Reminder pain in the physical realm is more straightforward. Tweak, pull, strain, tear, cramp, all momentary events which shout stop, something is wrong. Further, pain can spot specific or referral pain. A bulging back disc sends referral pain down the sciatic nerve into legs. A pinched nerve in the neck can produce tingling in the hands, fingers or outer extremities. Physical injury reminder pain flips a negative connotation switch. It just yells Stop. Conversely, stretching, yoga, increasing flexibility, range of motion is a positive pain pathway in that we know releasing, opening into new spaces is beneficial, even though uncomfortable pain.

Observing how pain is messaging our system produces pearls of wisdom, extremely valuable data points bolstering emotional intelligence. Where physical pain is often the most uncomfortable, mental and emotional pain can be equally debilitating, and prove more challenging to rehabilitate. Embedded in our fight or flight response patterning, tipping points in performance are created when things like *I just can't take this anymore* surface. This is a mind on strike, the brain front and center voice convincing us to give up. The mind has produced a thought construct which is a hologram, a projection of fear, an illusion. This is a mind under duress.

Here something in our physical operating system wants to move away from pain and towards pleasure, something less painful. What is the best and highest good regarding your choice? Stop or push through? Maybe pain is masquerading as fear or Anxiety. Something is being experienced that threatens our perceived ability to endure or survive. But one doesn't die from temporary pain. The human construct, mentally, emotionally, physically can endure levels of discomfort way beyond what mental chatter is screaming. It helps to be able to discern, tune in to your body.

The difficult piece in confronting, processing what generates emotional and mental pain, what is sourcing it, and why, bleeds into Freud's discussion of the ego, its role in our fight or flight responses, how the ego constructs and projects its importance. And where all things ego are necessary to delve into, it is complicated psychology to absorb and integrate. I say complicated because as a professional athlete, a fully functioning ego is critical to staying 'alive' at the top of the pyramid. While ego isn't necessarily a negative element, it's what the ego creates in mind chatter that can produce illusionary doorways we mistake as truth.

Is it just the torn ligament screaming, or is your ego scaring you by muttering, 'well, there goes your one chance'? There can be residual pain from rejection, past failure, or traumatic injury. While an athlete objectively deals with the pain embedded in physical progress or injury, we all confront subjective pain, the types of discomfort experienced which aren't the result of physical injury. Freezing under pressure, disappearing as a leader when times are tough, being told you aren't something, harassment or being suppressed is subjective pain. These create blockages in the psyche which can be painful to push through, move past.

Eons ago, in the days of Greek philosophers, Socrates, Plato, Pythagoras, et al, the dichotomy of a mind at rest and a mind under duress were given strict attention in the schools of wisdom. The school's methodology only imparted the sacred teachings, metaphysical tenets, and truths believed to be spiritual principles only after individuals spent time in physical regimens, training, and conditioning. It was taught that only through observing a suffering self, observing the content of mental chatter and its impact as a negative energetic influence, could the metaphysical teachings be fully absorbed and appreciated. The two sides of the mind, a survival mind, and ego-mind were reflected back to the individual for contemplation.

In the process, emotional intelligence heightens by separating illusion from facts. Reminder pain serves up an AMBER Alert that something has been jacked. Portal pain is more acute as we get dressed down in front of executives for a failed venture or serious shortcoming. Process the pain naturally. Pain management and subsequent pleasure behaviors can become unhealthy habits which create peripheral stress on other realms.

There is a lot of work we have to undergo to rehabilitate physical injury with success. One must participate in getting a system back into equilibrium. Dealing with mental or emotional pain is the same. Diverting, masking, attempting to numb it, get relief from the chatter through substances, additives or alcohol just muddles the pleasure-pain conversation. Portal pain, heeded with a spiritual attitude can take us into deep transformation.

In the Heart of all Matter

On a physical level, the literal pumping station of life's flow is the heart. On a metaphysical level, it is the creative (light) force. In metaphor, it is creation sourced from love. In the crosshairs of evolving spirituality and mindful physical action is the heart, the center point of all we are and do.

Conscious creation in physical activity requires the persona of an alchemist. Disciplining mind towards the positive, shaping emotional energy to focus on happiness inherent in our hearts, we build a stronger heart energy through respect, integrity, commitment, and right action. Energetically, this state of being promotes optimum flow.

The paradox of existence; it is and it is not. It could be a great performance, only to finish second. The greatest sacrifice you have ever made may have felt like it didn't meet expectations. The mind gives us its version, but the heart provides our truth.

Recall the infinity symbol is two circles (two zeros) attached. Each circle is metaphorically a complete system. One can be labeled our god system (metaphysical) and one our human system (physical). Force is present in perpetual motion traversing both spheres in equal distance. In our daytime existence, we are dominated by the physical realm. In sleep-time, we are in another realm, our subconscious, where if we direct our intention properly (e.g.—conscious desire) we can be in union with the unseen, the potentiality of all.

If you are vibrating in negativity, (fear or hate in the heart) the alchemy in your creation process will perpetuate that energy's vibration. If you are vibrating in the positive/creative, this is the essence of love, considered the strongest of all forces. Both are harmonic in nature, but the frequencies are different.

So how does this all relate performance and transformation? In the crafting of a performance vision, we obviously have a general construct of what the goal is; we are at point A and we want to achieve getting to point B. How we get there is of relative importance in that we do not know what twists and turns the path holds.

From a vision quest, identified is a vision of what we want to co-create. The emotional energy in this process is love, joy, determination, excitement in that we feel ourselves in a place to experience becoming the imagery we envisioned. You must love yourself and love the vision to calibrate the light force you are creating.

In a transformational capacity, we look at this process from its opposite side. When tested to a point of despair, we come to know/feel what we no longer want. The clarity of knowing something wholeheartedly. If we are tired of being angry about something, from a heartfelt place we want to cast harmony, joy, gratitude or love, opposite energy from that which is in place. If we are dreading something, the more we dread it, the more it attracts like kind. Like riding a bike; in adrenaline situations, we grip the handlebars harder.

Flipping your reaction script. Energetically amassing the opposite energy of what we experience displaces intensity of the opposing force. At those times when you feel you have done everything possible, now let go.

Breath and Breathing: Rhythm and Flow

The breath is a very powerful tool. Physical performance is optimized by working with our breathing; Oxygen, CO_2 and our red blood cells the elements for energizing or equalizing. Movement therapy is as much the science of breath as it is integrity in physical posture. Doing properly with less the guiding philosophy. As much about fueling our cells with oxygen, it is understanding breathing as life force feeding our body. If there is an imbalance of breath, there is a hiccup inflow. We seized, stopped or are sizing things up. In a quick moment of surprise, do you notice your breathing hold?

In passive form, we access the breath sequence to produce internal equilibrium, calm, balance or the sensation of relaxation. If breath cadence is monitored while active, there is the opportunity to harness its flow for sustained performance, energizing for peak burn or bursts of power. Following the breath sets the table for rhythm and flow. It can add fuel to the system or dissipate energetic blockages. Using the breath to establish cadence is where the physical system is in peak performance while balancing everything else in motion.

In balance, all systems respond in proper timing; all things are fluid and flow in a particular rhythm. Cadence is important because rhythm and flow dictate consumption of vital energy as well as how to manage the application of energy as a force. When things are in sync, so to speak, the process or action feels more natural, easier. When things are forced or controlled unnaturally, energetic buildup creates a feeling of agitation, uneasiness, and in extreme situations, breakdown. Slumps in sports can be characterized as a breakdown in technique and execution combined with low self-confidence, a negative core belief 'I just can't seem to do this right anymore.'

In our physical body, the dominant lever in achieving flow begins with the breath. If we speed up our breath, our pulse quickens; when able to slow the breath, consistently and methodically, heart rate slows. With physical output, the cadence in breathing produces a certain rhythm, which calibrates other functions necessary for exertion and force. Aerobic stress testing is one way this process can be measured and observed. In the more routine activity, toggling with lap speed during a one-mile run aids in the observation of the physical sensations induced by core breathing. There is a rhythm where we find our stride, so to speak.

In Yoga, physical postures are in conjunction with the science of breath. As energy moves through nodes (nadis), the breath is the tool for moving this energy. Paradoxically, the art teaches and shows that proper breathing isn't necessarily to produce force, rather to develop awareness of balancing forces through conscious push/pull, exertion while stabilizing.

If you practice yoga, you would notice this as the shaking/ light trembling experienced when challenged in a pose or getting into posture. This trembling is muscles, nerve impulses et al calibrating through release, trying to achieve a balance between the input of stimuli and output of torque.

Properties of physical law and natural law all involve harmonics: waves, frequency, and rate of vibration. Whereby the heart is the core machine of our operating system, the breath is our life force, with it our cadence and flow in all systems and processes we undertake daily. In meditation, brain waves change as attention is placed on the cycle of breaths, peak and exhale point. It is taught in transformative meditation practices our connection to the breath cycle is the link to our heart-center, awareness of our true expanse, potentiality.

If you are in a happy or good state of mind, there is lightness in the body. You are breathing easy. When you are in the presence of an angry person, that energy field is felt, restricting flow. Both have different effects on our breath cycle. If you take close notice, anger, fear or extreme negativity causes one to hold their breath, or disrupt a breathing pattern, interrupting cadence. This process is evident when we face emotions that create chaos. When we are relaxed, breathing comes softly, easily.

Whether meditating, competing, training, swearing, laughing, negotiating, debating, screaming, sobbing, whispering sweet nothings, frightened, singing or encouraging, there is flow or disruption in our breathing. If you find difficulty in obtaining a certain consistent output, explore through passive and acting breathing how you can speed up, or slow down, your flow in life.

Feedstocks and Fuel tanks

In physical form, the human body is essentially a balanced ecosystem. Input influences output; cause and effect to a high degree. Do X and accomplish Y. Training is basically fine-tuning the engine for efficiency and maximum torque. We fuel organically and inorganically. Water is vital to the vibrancy of all cellular systems. Food groups provide material that is broken down into nutrients the system utilizes to operate. Enzymatic efficiency is a strong positive as a result of eating fresh for fit and low fat/sugar foods.

On an atomic level, our bodies are comprised of organic particles, organs, byways, throughways, connectors, filters, and generators. At the cellular level, entities are opposite forces in balance, positive and negatively charged. For every quark, there is an anti-quark, in matter, anti-matter. There is constant attrition and regeneration. Billions of cells, subsets in a bigger picture where our main performance concern externally only cares about how fast I accelerate when I hit the gas.

From the inside out, we go. Atomic to surface physical. Carbon-based entities who require high volumes of water, animal and plant food stocks processing fuel for energy. While we don't necessarily manage the everyday output of our physical operating system, we must balance what we put in. But beyond food and water, there is air, our need for breath and breathing. There are physical foodstuffs we consume for energy, but also the energy we consume as our mind and emotions filter through sensory input we endlessly confront.

If food and water are the physical properties the body absorbs for proper functioning, air represents the metaphysical. Touch, taste, and feel the water. Alkaline or high pH is palpable. Air, not so much. A gulp of fresh air or a hit from an oxygen tank doesn't taste different. Breathing is a cycle, the functioning of our nervous system is an out and back signaling sequence, action and reaction. Consciously we eat and drink, subconsciously we are constantly breathing. Out of our conscious awareness, energetically our body is in perpetual motion. We are conscious of some things, not overtly aware of other things, yet all processes partake in perpetual motion. Our physical cycle of infinity.

When food, air and water are combined, physically humans are balanced in motion. Too much or too little is reflected in body signals. Discomfort or disease are systems inherently out of balance. If the machine, the engine isn't tuned properly, it bonks. If we synthesize the wrong grade of fuel, e.g.—nutrition, the physical system puts out dank exhaust. To be on point, mentally alert, confident, and eager, all forms of physical system feeding are aimed at balancing in everyday motion.

Feedstocks are the constant of water combined with the universe of nutritional requirements our body needs require. What types of food we consume influences basic vibration. Plant-based eating is more vibrant to the system; processed foods high in fats and sugars are low vibration nutrition.

Understanding organic versus processed, what sugar does to our cycle when introduced in large amounts, how does drinking, smoking, or ingesting chemicals affect physical development, training, and performance? These cause and effect loops, for the most part, are quantifiable, manageable. Fresh towards fit is a basic operating principle.

With all the emphasis placed on good nutrition in recent years, individuals have much better knowledge about how to fuel for endurance and performance. Conversely, obesity in America remains a plus-size problem. Regardless of where one weighs in, first and foremost, key barometers mirroring physical strength, endurance, and performance relates to higher self-awareness about what we consume as well as what we waste, literally and figuratively. Overconsumption is a luxury most enjoy. This is a macro-micro issue, individually and collectively as a society.

But there are other energy sources much less discussed which deserve mention. Energy is embedded in a variety of acts that don't involve breathing, eating or drinking. Listening to a motivational talk, using music to pump you up during training or before a competition, or reading literature by the masters. Inspirational teachings, stories, a mantra you softly repeat, a dance that you do. Musical vibrations move through us, impacting vibration. positive energy joining physical activity is higher octane fuel.

Exploring the proper mix for any given system is a process of learning, trying and shaping. The learning emphasis remains on exploring how best to fuel your machine. Is what you are putting into your body burning cleanly or emitting a dank smell? Do you know your blood type, what foods are best suited for your system? Even if you can't or don't cook, try making satisfying meals from scratch, with intention. Once a routine is cultivated, eating fresh is always a feel good.

From an early start in life and sports, I was forced to take control of my food preparation. Between a mother who wasn't a good cook, my own gigantic sweet tooth, feeding for proper competitive sustenance, then figuring out how to lose four percentage points of body fat in six months, learned over many years of fitness and training were subtle ways my physical body responded to various ranges of food, frozen or processed, to live (fresh) and vibrant (raw).

Eating fresh is by far the most expensive but yields the greatest health and energy benefits. Shopping and cooking fresh isn't the most efficient for time-challenged schedules but is most supportive for vibrant organ, brain, and tissue functioning. It pays to stretch a budget to buy fresh fish, farm to table greens, specialty goods. There are purveyors who are mindful in how they grow, raise, and harvest, and these days anything can be discovered through basic internet searching.

The other consideration in what we consume, what we allow into our system includes all external stimulus we confront. What we see, read, hear, feel merely in reaction to outside drama: death, dying, deceit, decay. High volumes of negativity in society and culture, stressful energies being absorbed, condensing us to a point where outer behavior is having to decompress, vent, react, meet, match or manage. Day by day it becomes a rinse and repeat process. We turn the squelch dial-up to tone things out and become numb.

Therefore, in our attachment to all things physical, both food/nutrition, pleasure patterns, and social media/information distractions, a more sacred relationship must be formed to all we consume. Gaining greater respect for what is put into our bodies is primarily accomplished by sacred separation. Going without for small to long periods of time provides healthy ego suffering through conscious sacrifice.

Performing in the 'Zone'

Being in the zone as an athlete is a beautiful thing. You can describe the experience to some degree with words, but can't convey the sensation, how it expanded consciousness for a mere span of hours. Across an infinite series of unique occurrences, everything is functioning without resistance. Whatever the competitive set in front of you, it is as though no one else is functioning on your level of execution, thinking, seeing, and doing. Many facets of the experience make it feel, ethereal, spiritual.

There is a very divine component to the flow, and what one experiences. Across a measurable span of time, performance in action feels like there are no obstructions, no major challenges to the execution of one's will. Nothing short of an unobstructed channel, it highlights the overlay of a spiritual component on the physical plane. Mind and emotion are not in the mix; it is a divine dance in perfect harmony producing a sense of wonder, awe, and gratitude when reflecting on what you felt, did and ultimately accomplished.

The literal humor in this statement is that being in a *zone* is **'z' one** moment when all the physical and metaphysical tumblers align. In the trillion combinations presented in a specific phase of time, your combination clicks and all doors swing open. Senses expand and movement in the x, y, z plane of three dimensions connects with grace and ease. You can't predict its arrival or when it will happen. You can't necessarily train for it as a specific event. It just happens. Everything just clicks and there is nothing anyone around you can do to slow you down.

The premise behind being in what they call 'the zone' is a very metaphysical experience. Over my fourteen years of competing and playing, I can only truly recall being in that space a handful of times. When I look back and ask myself why it didn't happen more often throughout life and competition, a couple of rationales speak to me.

First, it is a glimpse into the energetic field we all exist in. Mystics term it the sea of potentiality. It highlights the complex set of variables in life, for an individual in a specific moment compared to the environment around you; the quantum number of formulas all playing out simultaneously. Occasionally, your sequence comes up, and when it does, you are nothing short of being 'on fire' as they say.

Second, whenever in a phase of training, competing or doing, there existed a hyper-focus on preparing for something. This laser beam focus is diametrically opposed to just going about daily life, flashing your light, reacting and letting go. This said, there were days when things were just falling into place, thinking I was in optimum flow, but it didn't compare to when I was in competition against a field, or up against others all vying for the same brass ring in a specific event. There seems to be something about the consistent training of the mind and body, which increases the possibility of occurrence. It doesn't happen sitting around watching TV all day.

Third, the feeling was very comparable to a few spiritual apparitions I have experienced, a couple of these occurrences were written about in my first novel, *Life, The Spiritual Sport.* One of the more powerful is one I rarely share, and that came standing atop the podium, awaiting the medal ceremony to commence. Trying to hide my happy tears from teammates and outside eyes, I found myself closing my eyes, just thanking every person and every spirit guide for the experience. From a state of complete gratitude, suddenly the immediate world around me blanked out. Playing out on the back of closed eyelids was a stream of snapshots encompassing the entire range of my development years, all elements of what had brought me to that specific point in time. The slide show was accompanied by a narration voice revealing where there were reasons for things in the times where my negativity was strongest. The mumbles, murmurs, and rumblings of eighteen thousand spectators muted.

Compared side by side to immersive spiritual epiphanies encountered, I had similar physiological responses to what it felt like being in the zone while an athlete. How I moved, experienced time, could intuit thoughts prior to someone speaking, felt one step ahead of whatever was happening, or about to happen, felt like a separate, temporary reality.

All in all, it was a glimpse into what I call a higher state of consciousness or higher vibratory awareness. Some authors in the sports and energy space refer to the zone as being in perfect flow. While this is accurate, for me and what I experienced, it is beyond being in the physical flow. There is connectivity, full bandwidth at your disposal.

Whenever it came about, the zone phase never lasted for more than a day. In fact, in the twenty-four to forty-eight hours following an incident of 'being in the zone,' I actually felt depleted, drained, slower on the uptake, fuzzier than when compared to that heightened state of being. Almost like some kind of weird arrhythmic hangover.

It is a reminder that when we properly prepare, work through the pain, develop mastery of mental, emotional levers, fine-tuning our machine, anything can happen because everything is connected. It provides a taste of what is beyond the mundane appearance of everyday being and doing. It is mental, emotional, and physical now greeting the mystery of invisible energy systems, sprinkled with the effervescence of divinity.

JRx

Here in the physical circle of consciousness, blended into physical action and doing are the positive practices of channeling creative, positive thoughtforms, emotions, and electricity. Ciphering (discernment) between the constructive and the destructive influences shaping behavior, we train new patterns into reality.

Two disparate circles of consciousness, mind and emotions, teeter-tottering on a horizontal plane, striving for balance now must be integrated with the physical and energetic to craft higher level performance or transformation. If mental and emotional are the east and west points, x-axis, now there is a shift to the north and south points in our sacred geometry.

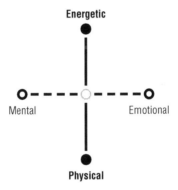

While the energetic grid function will be discussed next, there exists a blend of all the constants and their essences in physically becoming stronger and more efficient. The duality in performance and transformation shows that there are necessary attachments which are positive and constructive to becoming a better competitor. Obvious are positive perspectives, leveraging emotional energy into positive forces applied to change and doing.

Keeping the mind focused on a fixed goal requires siphoning out distractions and waste. Good nutritional habits are important to keep energy reserves high for physical action. Discipline in a progressive routine of strength and conditioning requires commitment and sacrifice. Understanding what we are physically attached to, and why, clarifies a perspective or position.

Discerning between positive and negative attachments is crucial to a solid foundation for growth. Healthy attachments are necessary for the physical realm of performance. The ebb and flow can be mirrored in the metaphor of rising, climbing, elevating. Discerning things, behavior, or patterns that are not for our best and highest good are cut away, sacrificed so to speak. Detaching from the pleasure-based attachments is a sacrifice in service to another, higher cause.

There is only so much room in one's competitive pack for items or elements that don't have high utility value. Keeping our machine in performance-ready condition is ongoing maintenance through attention and care. The more 'elite' one becomes, things that slow, hamper or distract are minimized or flat out discarded. There is no room for waste. What is consumed takes high priority as clean fuel without additives.

Respecting a challenge before you engage in the act of competition is a mindset of humility. At the heart of all your matters is a burning desire to become something. You see it. You dream about it. You want it. There is inherently a bundle of sacrifices to be made along the way. The prudent achiever doesn't travel the path shouting out his/her grand accomplishments at every weekly meeting. The conscious intention of separation, developing a sacred lens through which you will engage is the service work.

Give and you shall receive. It becomes a mindset of knowing your sacrifice but not making it about yourself. It's accepting the service work without expectations of what it will do for your ego. Respect for the overall process begins to take on a sacred slant. The balance of powers in motion.

JRxercise

The concession going into this exercise is acknowledging regardless of where we think we are, the stated goal is advancing, getting stronger, physically and metaphysically. What was gleaned from previous JRxercises, honing the interchange of thoughts and emotions, will definitely surface in the observation of how our physical system responds in performance and transformation/ change. This is a dualistic practice in that performance has us looking at our goals involved in bettering our competition, balancing creative and reactive with positive intentions. The other half involves separating from attachments, with a sacred intention, that helps us clarify our heart-center's power.

PERFORMANCE

Assessing, refreshing your game plan. Doesn't matter whether it's a sports goal or a professional objective. There are fundamental principles across both endeavors which structure the basic platform of building strength, or experience, and getting stronger. While it implies our body is getting stronger, there are metaphysical tenets to be practiced enabling more effectiveness, more efficiency in how you advance.

There are many avenues to research basic strength and conditioning, how the metrics reflect progress. A game plan for training where the goal is competition, sports or life, just reflects different variables in addition to the constants of consciousness. Science has us covered when dealing with our physical body, training, developing, or mastering levels of physical proficiency.

The objective in preparing is creating a core belief that you are entitled to an epiphany, the revelation of being 'in the zone.' This involves learning how to take your mind chatter out of the conversation. Taking inventory, assessing where you were, where you want to go, what you want to manifest requires updating the vision board. Imagery/visualization allow us to 'see' a finished product without blemish. Emotional energy in the form of love for what we are doing is bolstered by seeing things more objectively, less emotionally.

Key in this process is embedding intentional energy of 'doing what is for the best and highest good for all involved,' beyond thinking and doing in a self-centered capacity. This is expansionary energy which taps into profound components of sacrificing for the collective, being in selfless service, doing your role to your best and highest good for the benefit of all, without being dominated by personal wants and desires. Be bold. Be selfless.

Incorporating these perspectives into refreshing a particular vision takes our creation into a higher frequency of vibration. This motivation, intentional energy is then paired to the physical acts which we know will assist our physical body perform at a peak level. Next is looking at all that we consume, both in our feedstock (what we are putting into our system), as well as what we are 'consuming' from our external environment, information, news, noise, pollution, shock events, pressures of life and daily living.

If there is laziness around eating habits, for example, set a three-week plan to explore the positive opposite. Try consuming high vibration products: fresh wherever available even if it hits your budget harder. Explore juicing, pay attention to ingredient labels for packaged foods, replace white sugar with more natural sweeteners. If you are a habitual drinker or have other pleasure-based escapism activities in your routine, look for ways to reduce or confine how much you partake. Nutrition as good fuel takes more time and effort than a convenience store diet, but the effects will produce noteworthy moods of feeling lighter, brighter, and bouncier.

Regarding the noise that is consumed daily refine your intake to begin lessening the negative, dark or depressing stimuli. Be self-aware of pedantic behavior, gossiping, lying, where personal integrity is compromised by not doing what you say. Limit the divergent energies that affect our moods, be curious and explore illusory states of being. Don't get fixated on how many followers you have, or how many likes of your post. Don't engage in something to be liked; do something that adds value.

Last but not least is engaging in passive and active forms of meditative concentration, really staying focused on the breath cycle, breathing from the abdomen and not the chest. Traditions talk about not focusing our inhales and exhales from the chest area. Rather, the in-breathing should originate from a deeper place, lower belly. From there the breath is pulled up, peaking in the third eye, then emptying the out-breath through the lower belly, the Hara zone. It is a more elliptical rhythm.

Quell mental grinding by structuring the mind through consistent repetition in physical activity. Say a mantra 100 times while walking. Count your steps. Convince yourself everything is good and beautiful while doing the laundry or doing the dishes. If you are leading an active lifestyle, exercise with an imaginary spirit guide, someone only you can see and talk to running right along with you. Yell, scream, dance with your earbuds, channeling that angst, desire to burn something off. Hike into nature to ponder perfection, putting challenges and distortion in perspective.

TRANSFORMATION

Sacred Separation. Go without. Look within.

The prescription for clarifying attachments across a wide slate of conditions is straightforward, but admittedly painful. Full clarity, heartfelt truths, synthesize after a full circle analysis, from the light to the dark, positive to the negative. To better understand an attachment as positive or negative wisdom teaches, we must separate, 180 degrees away to an opposite pole. The energy involved in the attachment must be purified by temporarily cutting energetic tethers, clarifying our intention, motivation, or rationale, thus fostering a new perspective when re-relating or re-engaging, after going without for a phase of time.

This implies sacred separation. The act of separating is a sacrifice, in service. With a heartfelt intention, you are seeking truth. The important component in the process is quantifying intention. The more reverent the approach, the more all-encompassing the wish, more clarified is the heart energy. A deep intention to get something done, or die trying, is a cliché but drives the point home.

The vibration of love as a frequency is powerful. It's infectious. Sacrifice as a sacred act is reverence, putting one's self aside for a time to fully merge with a goal, all that must get done to create an opportunity. No one is going out of their way to help you. Not many people are going to give you any rice from their bowl. Cease applying the wrong type of force.

The supreme state of consciousness in achieving becomes an accomplishment reflecting the betterment of self wherein selfless service is a powerful force. Expanded awareness of the bigger picture is constructive for the entire community. Sacred sacrifice, acts of selflessness raise our emotional intelligence, build personal power, confidence, and self-esteem through positive suffering. The balance in thinking and feeling manifests as right action, a pyramid with perfect structural balance.

There are multiple substances promoting the expansion of consciousness, LSD, peyote, DMT, ayahuasca, Ppsilocybin, even certain sativa strains. All are currently being tested and applied in areas of behavioral therapy and science of mind relating to pain, consciousness, and awareness. Current research around LSD postulates that under the influence, information and stimulus don't fully process, it skirts around the thalamus creating distortion in other systems. Ayahuasca, a vine/leaf, is commonly used today by trippers seeking their truth. DMT is said to produce momentary separation in the psyche.

Purification rituals and practices should be approached with care and respect. It is recommended to have a qualified facilitator guide any fasting regimen. Having participated in extreme dry fasting multiple times (three-plus days of no food, no water) separating from that which you think sustains you, presents paradigm shifts in the psyche. And no, there are no psychedelics involved. Not to say tripping or micro-dosing is wrong. Nothing of the sort. But connect with the energy of the portal you are utilizing, and why.

From beginner to intermediate seeker types, very modest applications of sacred separation magnify our sensory awareness. But again, things you are used to, water, hugs, sugar, alcohol, vaping, pills, soda, or fast food, understand there is emotional pain experienced in the separation. Like the god Bacchus wanting to know why everyone just stops having fun being gluttonous, the ego will quickly add its two pennies of sense.

The intention motivating this exploration should be based on a heartfelt desire to expand beyond a certain state of being or feeling. In some spiritual traditions, enduring suffering in ceremony is done for all those who can't. It is done for all your ancestors and current family so to speak. This process of release will be met with pushback on multiple levels, physical, mental, emotional. Energetic shifts occur and these are highlighted in the following chapter. As we go without, it is from within we encounter many of our negative ego tendencies.

In shifting physical addiction, unhealthy attachments, self-limiting behaviors, there is a blend of reminder pain and portal pain. Our system perceives distress and all signals respond accordingly. This presents a perfect working environment to elevate consciousness by managing head trips and channeling our intuitive wisdom in any given situation.

By consciously separating from things you enjoy, are used to, or flat out need, we come to learn a lot about the mind under duress when our survival instincts are triggered. Ciphering the distortion ultimately aids in greater clarity. Do I really need this, want this? Why am I really doing x, y, or z? Is this really for my best and highest good? Do the uncomfortable and shock the senses. Our minds, bodies, and spirits, in acts of sacred sacrifice, can endure way more than both science and our ego tell us.

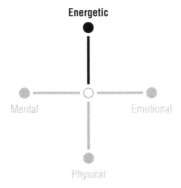

Energetic

Mental

Emotional

Physical

LIVING ENERGETICALLY

Rhythm, Frequency, and Flow

There exist three unshakeable categories universal in our experience which make up our reality fundamentals. These broad precepts, whether conceptual, theoretical, or definitive are base ingredients for any reality, event, or performance. The fundamentals of how we perceive, perform, and transform touch the following: 1) atomic/subatomic particles; 2) quantum physics (allows particles to be in two states at the same time); and 3) forces.

The first fundamental comes with a brief review of atomic and subatomic particles and properties. There are ongoing attempts by scientists to complete a model of the universe and its atomic functioning: the Grand Unified Theory, string theory, and the Standard Model used to explain particle dynamics.

Fundamental principles in particle physics, the Standard Model, came to light when scientists started colliding atoms and studying the resulting dynamic, from both structural and energetic viewpoints. What resulted was the identification of opposites in the 'universe,' as well as complicated explanations on how energy does not completely dissipate, but reallocates, shifts, moves, gets absorbed, attaching to other entities.

They explain to us there are fractional discharges of energy (decay), but for the most part atomic particles, the scientists report, show us that as formations get compromised, e.g.—disassembled, those same particles that went into forming a specific shape or entity with a specific energy structure become something very different when outside energies, charges, are introduced.

The Standard Model bases down fundamental components and their opposite counterparts: six quarks, six leptons, six anti-quarks, six anti-leptons, and the force carriers. Of these particles, quarks are observed in three pairs, each pair having their anti-quarks. The three pairs are termed as up/down, charm/strange, top/bottom.

In addition to quarks, there are six leptons (three of which have an electrical charge and three of which do not). The defining characteristics of quarks and leptons are that quarks are sociable and only exist in composite particles with other quarks, whereas leptons are solitary particles.

Further, what science tells us is that for every type of matter or particle, there has been identified a corresponding, antimatter particle (antiparticle). Antiparticles look and behave just like their corresponding matter particles, except they have opposite charges. For example, a proton is electrically positive whereas an antiproton is electrically negative. When gravity is introduced gravity affects matter and antimatter the same way because gravity is not a charged property, and a matter particle has the same mass as its antimatter.

Quantum physics has developed a vast array of applications producing our society's most dependable view of measuring physical matter in dynamic, resulting in wave theories of how matter performs. The paradox in quantum plays into this book dialogue because what has proven confusing to scientists is what is defined as the collapsible wave theory involving measuring matter and waves.

The paradox, by mere physical observation of measuring particle matter or wave experiments, how those entities function or operate is affected. Or in more layman terms, an observer can collapse a wave function just by observing. (If you haven't seen the movie *What the Bleep*, there is an animated vignette telling the tale of scientists' double-slit experiment). What is so huge about this conundrum is that there appear to be two laws of physical systems, one of measuring, and one of observing that produces two different experiences.

Third, revisiting the five types of universal forces in play for all of humanity (referenced in the overview pages) we hone some very sharp drill bits:

1. We can fully embrace the existence of duality as reflected that everything has an opposite counterpart, that energy transfers and affects matter.

2. How our tendency to measure things, predict behavior is directly influenced by our observations and perceptions as conveyed by quantum physics.

3. There are five types of (physical/energetic) force that influence change, performance, co-creating.

Energy and the Body Mind

Admittedly, it is difficult to think about physics while walking our path. The profound principles of science don't focus on the human energy system as a subset of the human body/mind. It is a system within a system. Shakti energy is the focus. Most cannot see this functioning although there are mediums and channels who see auras, energy fields. Primarily intangible, our energy field produces a vibration, a frequency, like a hum to a large outdoor power line. This energy also extends beyond the boundaries of the physical body. There is very much a micro and macro to our energy and how we 'are' out in the world. As within, so without.

The basics and the obvious appreciating our unique current can be witnessed in basic transference exercises. Watch a circle of people holding hands, introduce certain products that source energy, and watch the magic light bulb illuminate in one person's grip. Energy doesn't discriminate its users. It's the other way around. A source or conduit can be channeled or tapped. An act is performed with an energetic intention of love, or spite. Of primary importance is discovering the way to siphon from various power grids, external and internal, and convert that charge, flinting a heart-spark.

Energy packets arrive through each one of our senses, sight, sound, touch, taste, and feel. A sensation followed by a positive or negative slant. How we relate to an environment can be initially perceived as favorable or unfavorable. Losing streaks, slumps, lost deals, can't catch a break type of runs are as much a temporary breakdown in mechanics as it is loss of positively charged energy due to self-confidence sinking.

In addition to our external environment containing various energy sources, individuals have their own electrical grid to observe and manage. There is linkage to how we feel in our environment based on resonance. We vibe, get along with something, or it repels us. An urban lifestyle suits some more than others. Faster pace or slower pace mirrors like-kind energies.

Our external relationship to energy, the energy in things is often more tangible; our life force energy, more internal. Its existence and what that means more esoteric. This said, to more succinctly understand the energetic realm, how it is related and is tapped to maximize performance, an introduction to the subtle points in the bigger picture is necessary.

Western culture places much less emphasis on relating to our personal energy grid than eastern cultures. Meridians, nodes, nadis, centers of concentrated power called chakras, ley lines all exist and have significance. But since we can't actually touch, see or taste, generally we are not inclined to explore. The mind must compute there is 'intrinsic' value pursuing a practice of energy awareness.

Tapping into our grid is moving through layers, identifying and observing our most subtle of layers. Basic exposure to these embedded systems, appreciating how energy flows in and through our physical system, quickens our ability to shape performance. So much of performance and change is dependent on our energy stores being in rhythm and flow, not constrained and stuck.

Rhythm and flow promote a specific frequency or vibration. Laughing is lighter energy than crying. Darkness/evil is a lower vibratory rate than light/spiritual. Not feeling quite in step as you wake up in the morning could be a signal something is off energetically. Where and how we integrate all aspects of our mind/body with energetic influences determines how we are in the world. Creating is a choice. Ultimately, we choose to do this or that because it feels right. Something is vibing with our system.

In addition to scientific laws and principles discussing energy, how energy disperses, much less talked about are the fundamentals of natural law (or divine law). Natural law combines with physical law to influence how we perceive the potentiality of any given situation. Natural law governs the metaphysical properties of energy and energy exchanges.

Natural Law/Divine Law

Natural Law (NL) is a body of laws considered as derived from nature, right reason, or religion and is ethically binding in human society. NL reveals intention that the universe is in order, and that there are philosophical, scientific, and spiritual precepts which provide an overview of how that order comes to be. NL establishes power, functions, attributes, and phases throughout various planes of the universe.

The purpose of NL is to ensure a progressive and successive cycle in evolution, regardless of what obstacles man may create trying to interrupt their operation. NL is always constructive, even when it may be interpreted by a lack of understanding to be destructive. A pertinent subset of the overall list of natural laws important in the creative, heart-spark conversation encompassing energy:

Law of Attraction
Action suggested is that the creations of like vibrations tend to be attracted to each other. The attraction is considered magnetic in nature. As you think, so shall you become.

Law of Cause and Effect
Every action has an appropriate reaction. Dynamics of cause and effect cover similar action laws, retribution, and karma. Law

of Retribution states each of us receives according to what is earned; In karma, as a man sows, so shall he reap. A karma adherent may say that we can also live under karmic debts from the past. Law of Free Will, we are still free to choose how we will meet and pay those debts.

Law of Balance

The true meaning of equilibrium. The law commands that all actions of any nature between pairs of opposites in nature, or between man, must be balanced. Balance through counterbalance. Poise and power. Mental fortitude, strength is cultivated by striving to keep an even mind under all circumstances.

Law of Abundance

This law reflects one's ability to live in conscious awareness of the divine source of all things. Energetically aligned, from the heart-center, allows us to continually produce needs for the outer expression of our inner being. Knowing thyself, thus loving thyself, produces expansion, the potential to create.

Law of Love

The creative source and power of all life. Love is purifying. The realization of this law is the highest goal to be attained. The energy embedded in creation out of love is magnified power. Living in this law provides freedom from negativity, jealousy, hate, resentment, and revenge. The love principle is the action of giving and its reaction of re-giving. Spiritual motivation is based on love, the strongest of our five types of force and the highest vibration.

Law of Vibration

This law teaches that all things in the universe exist in a state of motion termed vibration. Vibration and matter compose the objects and forms in our universe. Rate of vibration dictates the form or state of being assumed. The energy in thoughts and emotions reflects general vibrational states of being, positive or negative. Intention is vibrational. There is a duality in the vibrations of anger and joy. Thoughts are things.

Law of Substitution

Akin to laws of desire, thought, and mind. Nothing is impossible for one that has the will to co-create life. If we accept negativity, poverty, lack and self-limitation, they will be ours. If we refuse, recognize the platforms of other laws, our vibration reflects there is no limit to the prosperity we can achieve as we can substitute anything positive for anything negative.

The Body's Electrical Grid

Highlighting this path work is getting familiar with the schematic of our internal energy grid. Energetic pathways are aligned with our nervous system. Tuning into 'rhythm and flow' is a process of cultivation because it takes time to appreciate the energetic push/pull of stimuli. It becomes necessary to decompress, so to speak, and the only way to get in touch with this is through stillness.

In Chinese medicine, acupuncture relates to energy flow or blockages with specific tracks in the body called meridians which influence all of organ and subtle system functioning.

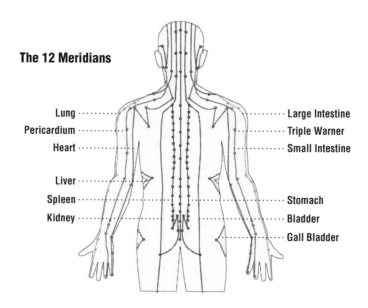

The 12 Meridians

Lung · Large Intestine
Pericardium · · · · · · · · · · · · · · · · · · · Triple Warner
Heart · Small Intestine

Liver ·
Spleen · Stomach
Kidney · Bladder
· Gall Bladder

In Hindu culture, the science of breath reflects three primary energy channels, ida, pingala and sushumna which dominate thousands of other 'switching station' points throughout the body. This is a mirror of the nervous system. Ida runs left of the spine, pingala right of the spine, sushumna, centered in our spine. The term kundalini is associated with the merging of all three energies flowing from south to north, up through the chakra grid (centerline of body).

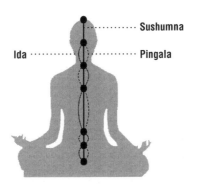

The Three Main Nadis

Dominant in Eastern philosophy is the system of chakras. Primary chakras are seven concentrated centers of energy, aligned north/south along our body's midline.

The first chakra, the root chakra, is located farthest south, the general area of the tailbone corresponding to approximately three inches down from our belly buttons (front zone of the body grid). The seventh chakra is the opposite spectrum, north, crown of the head. From the down below, to the up above, chakras each have a sound, color, and set of organs they influence.

The lower three chakras are more primal, our connection to earth, how we 'ground' to the down below. The upper three are considered more in the air realm, our divine influences received 'from above.' When the up above and down below are in balance, that merge activates the heart chakra, the metaphor of love.

Chakras are energy centers which collectively are a relational metaphor to our inner and outer worlds. In alternative medicine references, you may have heard someone comment, 'oh your throat chakra is blocked,' or 'your chi is out of balance.' These references relate to flow, open or congested portals.

These are the primary seven chakra references.

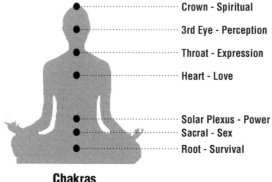

Crown - Spiritual
3rd Eye - Perception
Throat - Expression
Heart - Love
Solar Plexus - Power
Sacral - Sex
Root - Survival

Chakras

Christopher Kilham's book *The Five Tibetans* presents a comprehensive summary connecting the significance of chakras. The channels run from the base of the spine to the top of the head, conveying energy from one chakra to another. Sushumna, the central channel, is the energetic counterpart to the spinal cord and is the core channel of all energetic flow in the human energy system. Sushumna is the primary pathway through which energy flows from the base of the spine to the top of the head.

Kundalini energy travels through the sushumna, illuminating body and mind. The origins of sushumna and the other primary energetic channels, ida, and pingala, are at the base of the spine, the location of the root chakra. Ida runs up the left side of the central channel; pingala ascends the right side. These two channels travel upward, intertwining with each other at each chakra. Their physical counterparts are the ganglionic nerve chains that run alongside the spinal cord. Ida is connected to the left nostril, and pingala is connected to the right. *Ida* is considered lunar in nature, while pingala is regarded as solar.

For old-schoolers, recall the early television advertising using the caduceus by the American Heart Association (the doctor's symbol—the Rod of Asclepius, the ancient mythical god of medicine). It is a representation of the three major energetic pathways. Depicted as a staff with two serpents winding around it, and a pair of wings on top, the caduceus symbolizes the ascent of consciousness, from lower chakras to higher ones. The wings of the caduceus represent the two-petaled third eye, the wisdom eye, or eye of revelation.

The Seven Primary Chakras

First Chakra

The first chakra is located at the base of the spine at the perineum, the spot on the physical body between one's anus and genitals. The energy flowing through this chakra is dense, vital, and powerful. This chakra is the closest to Mother Earth and deals primarily with the lowest vibration energy. This chakra is associated with all basic aspects of human survival, very primal energy. It is the root of our consciousness, thus corresponding location at the root of our spine.

Primary functions:	survival, power, vital life energy, courage, elimination, awakening of kundalini energy
Associated color:	red
Associated organs:	large intestine, rectum
Associated glands:	adrenal glands
Associated sound:	LAM (sounds like Lamb)
Related nerve center:	coccygeal, sacral plexuses

Second Chakra

The second chakra is located just below the navel area, slightly above the reproductive organs and is fundamentally associated with creativity. Creativity is also seen here in the form of procreation and regeneration of which sexual energy is a core component of these actions. Sexual energy as creative force includes thoughts, feelings, behavior, dress, and when channeled intentionally, promotes creative expression including, but not limited to, art, music, fashion, design. It is an all-pervading force.

The second chakra is a highly active center, the energy of which permeates virtually everything we do. It is fundamental to both basic creativity and higher ecstasy. The negative aspect of second chakra energy is that we can get 'stuck' in this primal, sexual force energy. In depiction, the second chakra is the zone of 'Hari Kari,' death by dishonor.

Primary functions:	creativity, procreation, sexual function, promotion of vitality, force
Associated color:	orange
Associated organs:	large intestine, bladder, kidney, sex organs
Associated glands:	reproductive organs
Associated sound:	VAM
Related nerve center:	prostatic plexus/vaginal plexus

Third Chakra

The third chakra, located at the solar plexus, is considered the center of the individual self. This center deals with expression, the individuation of consciousness that extends beyond basic survival. Energetically, the projection of self as a unique being in a unique expression. It is the center of personal power and the origin of will. This chakra generates the drive toward self-assertion, personal determination, and individual strength, preparing us to meet the challenges of living in the world. The center can be enormously powerful and is associated with personal charisma.

Primary functions:	will, personal power, digestion, assimilation of nutrients, understanding
Associated color:	yellow
Associated organs:	liver, spleen, stomach, small intestine
Associated glands:	pancreas
Associated sound:	RAM (sounds like Rohm)
Related nerve center:	solar plexus

Fourth Chakra

The fourth chakra lies at the point of the spine behind the sternum, center of the chest, and is considered to be the focal point of love and compassion in the human energy system. It is at the fourth chakra that human consciousness moves beyond self-centeredness into an expanded awareness of connection with the rest of the world. At the midway point between the lower three and upper three chakras, the fourth chakra marks the point of conscious departure from lower to higher awareness.

The energy that flows from this center is directed beyond personal importance to consideration of others. To gain access to the higher functions of creativity and awareness, one must 'pass through' the fourth chakra. This is the metaphor dealing with the heart; the fourth chakra is the transformation from primal, material-based actions, desires (through the heart, the love aspect), to higher, more esoteric, spiritual considerations.

Primary functions:	love, compassion, immunity
Associated color:	green
Associated organs:	heart and lungs
Associated glands:	thymus
Associated sound:	TAM
Related nerve center:	cardiac plexus

Fifth Chakra

The fifth chakra is located directly at and behind the center of the throat. Through this chakra flow the energies for the higher functions of communication, creativity, verbal expression. The power of this chakra center is most notable in the activity of speaking. If oppressed, this is finding your voice. When the fifth chakra is strong, one can speak with tremendous force and persuasiveness. Expressions will be dramatic, powerful, and deeply moving. This chakra is so potent that its force can be hypnotic.

Primary functions:	communication, truth, expression
Associated color:	blue
Associated organs:	vocal chords

HEART-SPARKING PERFORMANCE

Associated glands:	thyroid
Associated sound:	HAM (sounds like Hom)
Related nerve center:	pharyngeal plexus

Sixth Chakra

The sixth chakra symbolizes our psychic center and is located roughly behind the high point of the nose, between the eyebrows and inward toward the center of the brain. Also known as the third eye, or wisdom eye, this chakra is the location of higher intelligence and clairvoyant vision.

The third eye is the center of insight, an inner vision directed by wisdom and a deep understanding of the subtle forces at play in any situation. Individuals with this extraordinary vision are the few true clairvoyants, whereby the higher intelligence viewed by this fully activated chakra is expansive and intelligent. An open third eye also enables one to easily achieve desired outcomes that are positive and generative.

Primary functions:	insight, higher intelligence, clairvoyance
Associated color:	indigo
Associated organs:	brain
Associated glands:	pituitary
Associated sound:	AUM
Related nerve center:	cavernous plexus

Seventh Chakra

Located at/on the top of the head, this chakra is commonly referred to as the crown chakra, portal of cosmic consciousness. Directly opposed to the primal energy and position of the first chakra, the root chakra (earth vibrations), this chakra is positioned as a funnel for all things from the heavens, celestial vibrations. It is an unconditional state of total fulfillment, the embodiment of total freedom, wisdom, energy, insight, and joy.

Upon awakening the seventh chakra, one finds that cosmic consciousness is the natural human condition. Such awakening is usually the product of intense purification, inner refinement, and spiritual work; however, since cosmic consciousness, or illumination/enlightenment, cannot be known by the intellect, one cannot say that there are only prescribed ways to attain this condition. The truth in genuine illumination can only be known through direct experience. In chanting the sound of 'OM' is related to deep meditation, signifying gratitude for one's life.

Primary functions:	cosmic consciousness
Associated color:	violet/white
Associated organs:	brain
Associated glands:	pineal gland
Associated sound:	OM
Related nerve center:	cavernous plexus

JRx

For novices, getting acclimated to the feeling of proper flow requires assessing energetic rhythm and flow. Tuning our energy is consciousness focused on the subtle mechanisms and metaphors of these pathways and portals. Developing awareness assists in keeping our flow vibrant and potent.

Similar to exercises in prior sections, getting in touch, so to speak, is facilitated by a variety of exercises one can perform while in solitude, or with some mindfulness even in the throng of hustle and bustle. Even in a professional setting or office, put some 'me time' on your calendar, as setting aside thirty minutes can accomplish much.

Because we go about our day in an environment bombarded by stimuli, pressure, demands, and timelines, it can be difficult to check in energetically. When planning a sit down with yourself, tack on five minutes to balance out the mind with some breath work, transitioning your focus and attention to whatever exercise or regimen you choose.

Following are recommendations to cover what I consider the two halves of the energetic whole. It helps to establish some baseline practice or experience for the three pathway categories, meridians, nadis, and chakras.

Meridians

Meridian work is slightly more intricate; however, to best experience I find licensed practitioners of acupuncture, Reiki and Qigong or Falun Gong to provide an array of teachings. If you choose to try acupuncture, anticipate arranging three sessions across three weeks. Without seeking therapy for a specific 'condition,' ask the doctor to perform a general balancing with commentary on what he/she culls from the diagnosis. Often during sessions, meridian activation will induce light muscle twitching along its pathways, generally in line, but sometimes in the opposite direction of needle placement.

If you don't do acupuncture, then try a Reiki master session. Here it would be more akin to a massage therapy session, most likely a practitioner will incorporate a massage table whereby you could be lying down, or in combination sitting and standing, depending on how their work is structured. Receiving this type of work can feel very relieving, feeling lighter, less congested. One should be able to just check in how the body registers different types of connections.

Qigong, Falun Gong embodies movement therapy and patterns, 'poses' that open our energy flow. Gathering, releasing, being mindful, diligent through a variety of smooth movements assists in promoting 'flow.' At times it may feel like you are blending martial arts moves and Pictionary in slow motion, but results from a good session with a good teacher are tangible.

Nodes and Nadis

Nodes and nadis, there is a specific nostril based breathing exercise which has three mini parts to reflect the three pathways. This exercise is best done with feet touching the floor, legs not crossed, sitting upright in a chair.

Using the forefinger, breathing is directed through the nose three ways.

First, alternate side nose breath. Place forefinger on one side, left or right, lightly pressing nostril closed. Breathing in through the opposite side, once at the inhale peak, release and move the finger to shut the nostril you just used, exhaling to the opposite nasal pathway. If you start by pressing the right nostril, you will inhale left, then exhale the breath through the nose on the right side. Then start opposite side from how you started and repeat. This should be done six times.

Second, same technique, but do not switch sides for inhale and exhale. Stay to the same side. Breathe in left, exhale left. Switch to the right side. Breathe in right, exhale right. Six times.

Third, without using finger pressure to close a nostril, breathe deeply (from belly, not chest), inhaling through the nose specifically, exhaling through the mouth from the belly. Full inhale, and full exhalation. Six times.

Chakras

Chakra exploration involves two modes of practice, one incorporating colors and one incorporating vibration through chanting a sound.

Referring to the list of attributes for each chakra, there is a color assigned to each, and a master sound, e.g.—TAM, OM, RAM, etc. First pass I suggest color therapy, whereby you will utilize your dominant hand to perform some circular motions (clockwise for front of body) over each chakra location. Conversely, color therapy can be accomplished through the installations of flowers, the corresponding chakra color seen in a specific flower. The root chakra, red, for example, could be a vase of red roses for that week. The second chakra, orange gerbera daisies, etc.

Re-read what each chakra represents, then in sitting meditation, bring up the color, keeping red for example in mind's eye, simultaneously using your dominant hand to create circular motions while not touching your skin. This motion combines imagery and action to bring each center to attention while also fostering flow in the portal, keeping the chakra 'open' and functioning properly. Sit for as long as desired, but a minimum of five minutes on each portal, color. Pay attention to images or things that surface in your thoughts and visions.

The other mode is using vibration, vocalizing the sound listed for each chakra. Starting at the base (root chakra) hold the respective color in mind's eye, then hold the sound over the entire breath out loud. Inhale, hold Red in your vision, then exhale saying 'Lam' out loud, slowly but diligently. Repeat three times for each chakra, moving up the body. (There is an alternative mantra that will follow the five phonetic vowel sounds (e.g.—Ah, Ay, E, Oh, Ou, where each is held until breath runs out. Ahhhh, then Ayyyyy, then E, Oh, Ou).

• • •

The other side of energetic exploration involves movement and tapping into places of power in nature. Considered more of a macro sensation affecting the body's state of being. By blending in a little fun and respect, deferring to the grandeur of nature, we can recharge our batteries. While we play in nature, we also go into nature with reverence.

Setting the tone in this piece asks you to play with a little music and dance. By yourself is preferred; the decibel level as loud as you feel it needs to be. From your all-time musical memory archives, pull forward a favorite song that would always get you bouncing and singing. You can add a little flare and identify yourself as a person in the band, drummer, singer, guitarist, frontman, or diva.

Karaoke for one, please. With the song, air instrument your performance, lip-syncing with passion. Belt out the tune, the lyrics, and meld into your performance. Encourage your body to move in intuitive rhythm with the flow and beat. Get your groove on, and make it a performance to inspire. By the time you are done, hands high overhead celebrating with the imaginary crowd eating up your every twitch and move, smile and feel the energy course through your system, uplifting and heart-sparking.

Give this performance a few days of charging your spirit, then morph into an opposite realm experience. This round is going into nature to commune with a place of power. Waterfall, wildflower field, huge old-growth redwoods, hiking to a destination, smells, sights or sounds. Pick your spot and plan a dedicated outing whereby you will set an intention for the connection prior to embarking.

The intention is a heart-centered desire for yourself or someone else. Call it a prayer or a sacred ask, this is between you and the outdoor spot you choose. There are a couple of suggested additions to your routine. First, set the intention the night prior so it stews in your fabric, seeps into your psyche. Second, incorporate some sacred separation. Make some type of pledge that the spiritual quest in which you are sacrificing, is something that lifts your spirit. Most obvious on the list of sacrifices, snacks, and water.

The goal is to not make the destination too difficult, too far away, because there are a couple of quiet forces that will go into your quest. Sacred sacrifice may be to abstain from drinking water until you return. This doesn't mean you can't bathe in the creek, shower under the waterfall, or wipe cool dew on your face. It just adds a parameter of doing something that is not about yourself. It is uncomfortable to fast, especially during light to medium exercise.

There is some level of discomfort, possibly pain. But this is portal pain, a doorway to a more fulfilling state of being as you need to always spin your challenges into positives. The quest is not time on the path to complain about your discomfort. There is a destination, whereby you will commune in quiet, just absorbing the grandeur of your place of power.

With all five senses, be inspired through each. Find a smell that is amazing. Make a bouquet of wildflowers, touch something that looks beautiful to you. If you know your outdoor edibles, pick something to savor, an herb, dandelion, sweet grass, cool clear water, wild mushrooms. If you are abstaining from water, then leave the taste sense as part of your fasting sacrifice. Channel energies through other neural ignitions. In nature, we seek to tap that which we can't tap in urban settings. It's a reminder that our life force, when in balance, has symmetry, but that we must pay attention to its maintenance and regeneration.

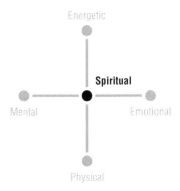

THE FIFTH CIRCLE, CREATING SPIRITUALLY

Metaphors and a Map

When an elusive concept or truth merges with our conscious understanding in any moment, an epiphany is experienced. Major or minor, epiphanies are those mystical moments in life; instant clarity suddenly achieved when disparate dots are simultaneously connected in our field of understanding. Instant context, meaning is exposed in between the packets of streaming thought. Epiphanies, magical as they seem, can be prepared for, but not predictable in terms of when they burst into view.

Kind of like being in the zone, as a competitor. An infrequent happening where everything just clicks, you are operating in what feels like an alternate reality. No one can stop you, in and of itself, humbling. But there is also something mystical like a proverbial veil was temporarily lifted providing a peek at divine functioning. Mesmerizing and mystical, it commands reverence for the Sufi proverb 'that which transpires behind that which appears.'

Behind that which appears on the surface are all the topics explored up to this point. We have physical and metaphysical systems working in tandem that we can control, manage and leverage. But at what point does it transcend from all things mind, body, emotions, and energy to a spiritual experience? Further, does evolving, raising our levels of consciousness imply we are living a more spiritual life?

Divinity, seeing things as divine, expands our capability to answer prior lingering questions. The externalization of a supreme being places man in a position to give thanks for the bounty or cry out in chaos when we need to blame a cause for whatever results we dislike. Again, a choice, but a choice which illustrates inherent separation.

In acts of service or sacrifice, purpose can be discovered in conscious submission. Gratitude as a perspective is heart-based humility for all the positive and negative. The substance of our lives, reality, ongoing processes of trying to control our lives, but also the art of letting go. Things we can explain and those things we cannot explain. We have our man part and our God part. Dual realities.

In the subset of two seemingly mutually exclusive circles, our man part and our god part, is where we create our heart-spark. The epiphanies, the new truths, new awareness, your new normal are occurrences in what I call the 'rendezvous sequence.' The moment when we can consciously drive creative action, thus joy from heart-based decisions and desires.

Where actions are not dictated strictly by cognitive processes, how we do what we want to do takes on different meaning and significance. When sacrifice is a sacred act because of the intentional energy embedded in said act, this is action which defines spirituality, doing for others. It is the transcendence out of physical hardship you didn't think was possible because your ego was screaming stop. The experience of thinking, seeing something, imagining it to become reality because you so desire it to be, is where we are divinely co-creating in heart-sparked performance.

In the matrix of force, we comprehend the energetic power of spiritual motivation, intentions. When someone says, 'now, put your heart into it,' you can understand and react, in command and with integrity. This is the giving up of one's thoughts based in self, expanding into how to create value for the collective.

My play on words contradicting there is no 'i' in team. 'I' team is where there exists a very grounded sense of self. Feeding yourself properly imparts the energy to help sustain others. Open and willing to do whatever is necessary to build the proverbial arc, whether captain or bench player, team manager, division executive or commander in chief. This is the realm where the physical goes metaphysical. The journey and exploration take you into a new place of power and performance; the heart-spark of ignition firing up creation.

Consciousness and Time

Ah, time and infinity. A conversation that could go on and on deep thru day and night. The space and time continuum that constitutes life, aging (and evolution), mirroring back there is no definitive end-point in its loop. Applying the infinity symbol to our time on planet earth, it represents two halves, two circles with a midpoint, in perpetual motion. Time framing up billions of interactions and exchanges. Convergence, raising consciousness is extrapolating out how our five realms contribute more when they mesh.

Each circle of consciousness, mind, emotions, physical body, energetic grid, while wondrous mechanisms, are not synonymous to being spiritual. Life force has divine properties, but doesn't define spirituality. Spirituality as a core belief blends in the fact that the whole is greater than the sum of individual parts as it relates to force and energy. It can be synonymous with God, or not.

What is spirit and spirituality are very personal compass points. It can be dogmatic, prophetic, religious, pagan-inspired or influenced by iconic deities. Whereby spirit can refer to entities, it is also life force, inherently divine consciousness. Spirituality, reflected in spiritual teachings are the platitudes of gratitude, integrity, right action, sacrifice, giving and receiving, from a place equating heart joy to divinity.

A spiritual path is one dedicated to merging physical truths, internally to externally, which includes the metaphors of as above, so below and as within, so without. Infinity, how we relate, manage perspective, and defend or create while in perpetual motion.

Man Part	*God Part*
Earth	Etheric
(At)tention	(In)tention
Mental/Physical	Emotional/Energetic
Performance	Transformation
Yang	Yin
Down Below	Up Above
Self, Internal	Beyond Self, External

To execute a shapeshift of perspective, take the two separate circles and mash 'em together. Not a trashy mash, but a stylish one. Make a fashion statement on your interpretation because the ask is to create and 'C,' a pair of shades. See something familiar in a new way. Shades with new lenses, new hues for how you capture images, relate to the outside world. Remember, the challenge is to truly see things differently.

The lenses of your new glasses have some unique features. Glare, so to speak, is influenced by core programming, files influencing how you interpret what you take in. Holding space for the duality in everything, perceived positive and negative aspects categorize our perceptions. Add the five constants, influences of duality, energy, force, equilibrium and geometry, performance becomes an art project crafted through discipline, passion, and expansion, designed with sacred purpose.

The fifth circle of consciousness houses our spiritual definitions and experiences. It becomes a process of performing to a higher level because now we have the tools to support physical growth (our man/woman part), leveraging with metaphysical knowledge (our God part). This is the realm where our concept of life, how we impact life, our footprint, transcends from mundane to magical.

To prepare a conversation on spirituality, why this is important in understanding and maximizing performance across any type of competition, starts with a command, not a quest. Namely, the command to consciously shift perspectives, staying open to the literal and the figurative. Developing a spiritually based way of being does not imply one becomes a doormat, extending buddha blessings to all as they climb their way over you. You define what it means, not others.

Understanding we are way beyond two-dimensional requires three-dimensional viewing. It requires a change, a transformation. This is the significance of 'Meta' in metaphor (Greek meaning 'to change'). In this meta(phor), it literally signifies the change from *phor* (4) into *phive* (5). This point becomes how we invisibly project into the world. As with metaphors in general, it has dual meaning.

An imaginary hologram, activated when we blend the four, core circles of consciousness properties with purified, positive energy. Putting on your new shades, view the realms as they have been listed, north, south, east, and west circle points on the body map. Imagine when you place attention on each circle, that realm lights up, a spotlight beam activated. When the four corners are activated and balanced, the fifth beam of light is activated. Four points, four beams projections up and out, converge into a single laser beam.

Acknowledging and respecting what you don't know can be as valuable as that which is clear and certain. Operating in the core belief anything is possible requires trust subconsciously. Trust that what you seek in the wisdom generated by heart, not mind. Notice as you go about your path where the mind seems to have produced as very real 'reason' to do something, but there is agitation (doubt) somewhere in the gut or body. Very subtle, something just not right, and not directly explainable.

Specifically generating a heartfelt purpose is different than a mental conviction you are, or are not, something. This requires our personal browser have a heart dominated homepage versus a redirect to another portal. Challenging is the training to shape positive tendencies. Sometimes we feel pushed into exploring the spiritual way because we are out of physical options that satisfy mind.

Establish a consistent communication pattern with spirit. In your personal dialogue (your prayers) literally ask for guidance, clues, help.

Ask and you shall receive.

Preparing for an Epiphany

Major or minor, epiphanies are those mystical moments that occur in life; instant clarity drops into our field of understanding that is just truth. I have found these messages generally drop in when I am not looking, focused, or grinding on matters we ponder, contemplate and obsess over. Epiphanies drop in between the gaps of streaming mind chatter. You must prepare accordingly for the experience to happen.

Those moments quietly gasping 'oh my God.' The intuitive truth drops in when dealing with challenge, frustration or despair. When it is most needed to elevate our spirit, our higher self-heard our request for help and is responding. Like mystical wind in our sails when we have been stuck dormant in the water, waiting or trying to make sense of the non-sensible. Do not dwell on why there is no wind, learn how to generate wind.

A spiritual path is directly correlated to one's energetic attunement. Our operating frequency is a harmonic vibration; we vibrate from low to high. It is this vibration which forms the invisible magnetron which attracts other matter or perpetuates patterns in our system, mind, and body. If we are looking to move out of, or beyond limitation, it is imperative that we raise our frequency.

Everything in us and around us has a vibe. We hear, feel, or sense it in sound, through word, nature, places which inspire us, via colors. All vibrations have a cadence that is generally a constant as it would relate to harmonics. Wind moves, fire burns, earth holds, light warms, and water flows. Rocks, people, music, anger, love, animals, trees, flowers, stars, prayer, spells, air, all hold a specific vibration, interpreted and absorbed differently depending on our energetic frequency.

When we move observation beyond the mental, emotional, physical realm, we then address the esoteric components of what we are as an organic container, and how that container affects and is affected by our environment. The harmonics of our frequency have a rhythm and a flow. When we notice something is out of balance, the first line of remedy is to discern energetically what is going on, creating to expand, or calibrating to pull back.

Harmonics, rhythm, and flow are integral when performing and transforming. Capturing the inherent power in this sequence is how we take things to a higher level. In our natural state of power, the equation is in balance; when we struggle, are down, or faced with trials, tribulations or tests, it takes effort to fine-tune a vibration.

The important byproduct of tending to our energetic field is that it allows epiphanies to enter into our flow like a step added to a dance. Thus, preparing for an epiphany is focusing our intention on what we don't know cognitively, yet seek to understand. Whether sports or spirituality, the elements are the same: intention/goal, preparation, construction, action, giving, receiving, and integration. This is the circle for all that we do, and how we create in the cycle, the circle of life.

Preparing for an epiphany is the observation and fine-tuning of each realm as it appears in our field of consciousness. Quieting the mind, taming the ego, chanting during a walk; writing, sitting in the sun, listening to the rain, wind, staring into and meditating on the power of grandfather fire, all facilitate a heartfelt intention for the world to receive our private communications and desires. It is the art of mindful choice, and how we thrive in any environment to align with that which we want to actualize.

Platform 14

The metaphor map as I call it, Platform 14, was born from a personal need to objectify, containerize principles I learned in sports performance but was difficult to separate into tangible practices when confronting major transformation in my life construct.

For instance, when I was eighteen, hearing mind, body, spirit, I could only focus on two of the three concepts, mind and body. But there I was, a budding athlete with a high burn, high torque personality. There was lots of emotional fuel but I had no idea how to cipher, do the work to separate the real from the surreal. So much time is spent following commands in life we tend to get distracted focusing on manifesting our inner vision.

I needed to get out of my head and create a construct that made sense, e.g.—rational. One that I could see, digest, be reminded every time I walked out of my bedroom to face another competitive situation. I had consumed many philosophical tenets but needed a simple representation that would trigger a positive feedback response in my state of being. As such, what evolved was geometrically framing the content with the reminder it's all about how you relate to the process.

The five realms, our circles of consciousness each contains stuff that benefits from oversight. When the mind is under extreme duress, the cognitive output process wobbles, is all things that frustrate. The reminder is the collage of all vista points along a traversed path; to walk it versus thinking about walking it. Ultimately, until events convince me otherwise, I believe there is a need for consciousness to be more pervasive. If we can all create to a higher level, especially when it appears our planet and its populations are under duress, then it is time to shift into overdrive.

As such, for tangible reminder reasons, I started manipulating data points, adhering to physical or metaphysical truths. The construction of the metaphor map has much figurative meaning.

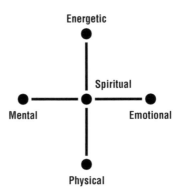

The placement of mental, emotional, physical, energetic and spiritual (heart) are not random. Mental and emotional circles are positioned on the horizontal for specific reasons. The circles of physical and energetic have guiding logic as well. The overriding metaphor, one primary point is activated when the other four are calibrated and channeled in positivity. With all we can explain, and not explain, the pinnacle point lights up the sacredness of integration.

Whimsical but rational, the map continued to guide me through great treks and murky waters. In fact, in crystallizing the content for writing this book, what you are being given was personally applied across each phase of this project. The master intention remains to create a short and sweet guide map for the best and highest good every individual can actualize.

Everything comes to a point.

The Reference Points in Metaphor

On the Meyers-Briggs scale, I represent the intuitive thinker. My style looks to assign meaning. Not as a random action of OCD, but from an analytical view that combines the 'out there' with the 'here and now.' Processing what I knew (objective), asking spirit for clarity about what I didn't (subjective), a straightforward application helped me sketch a performance reminder map. Some days it was about getting basic life functions accomplished. Other phases, it helped to prepare for a try to the top.

Leonardo da Vinci's "vitruvian man" drawing dropped in one day while meditating. There was a push to ponder his depiction of man geometrically. I set about finding anywhere in his work renditions relating man to the cosmos, any labeling that might have linked philosophy and body knowledge. Subsequently, it was looking for any mathematical associations or representations that might click.

I started asking friends to subject themselves to a quick experiment measuring distances being assigned to how I would depict the realms. Subjects were shown a picture, asked to stand in a style similar to how the Vitruvian man is depicted, arms out, legs slightly apart, chin up. Instructing subjects to bend left and right elbow towards their chests while looking straightforward, seeing where they touched reflected a base motion across all. I set that spot as center spot. As you might envision, it was center chest plate, mid-sternum.

Measuring fourteen inches to each direction from that center spot highlighted compelling body spot relationships. Fascinated, I went on to measure a blend of twenty-four other adults, mix of ages, heights. Bodyweight had no bearing, nor did gender, but all subjects were over twenty-one.

From a five-foot, twenty-six-year-old female, to a six-foot-five-inch former athlete at forty-five, fourteen inches (+/- .25 inch) all measurement points landed on identical body spots. For some reason, I assumed there would be some discrepancy between a five-footer and someone eighteen inches taller. The first responder chatter in my brain, odd that varying heights, ages, and genders would map the same. I couldn't get my mind around this at first, but I went with it.

The north circle, energetic, corresponded with the location of the sixth chakra, considered the third eye. Just above the bridge of the nose, between eyebrows, slightly up. Color representation for this node is dark blue and is considered the location we consciously synthesize etheric, spiritual energies.

Measuring to the south of the touched chest point, landed on the location of the second chakra, (approximately two inches below the belly button). Related, this spot is where the Asian act of Hari Kari (honorable death) is performed. This area represents the duality of honor and shame, grounding purpose. Color representation is orange. It is the synthesis point of earth energy (root chakra), our connection to earth, all things physical.

Interesting with these data points is manipulating their representations, blue (sixth chakra) and orange (second chakra) blend to green (heart, fourth chakra). Halfway between chakra six, and chakra two, is the fourth chakra, the heart-center. Metaphorically, it is in our heart-center where we divinely process the convergence of the down below and up above energies.

Next, measuring from center chest point to either side of outstretched arms, the tape landed on a spot just above the elbow (two inches north of joint), basically where bicep and tricep tendons attach. Physically the push, pull levers of action, perfectly mirroring the push/pull in mental and emotional functioning. Seeking meaning revealed coincidental meaning. Blend the Eastern philosophy tenet that our dominant side is our push side, non-dominant side is our receiving side, the mental circle of consciousness was placed on the body's right side. The corresponding energy on the teeter-totter, emotional circle, horizontally opposite Left.

When all five realms are balanced and functioning towards peak performance, all the light beams shooting up and out could be leaned and merged, similar to the point on a teepee. The peak point of a pyramid where there are four cornerstone points forming a fifth point. Activating heart energy, wisdom, and power, a hologram was born.

There was magic in the map. Fine-tuning each life situation and/or challenge, I approached knowing how to apply the physical and channel the metaphysical to generate output exponentially greater than when all circles of consciousness are left to their own, unattended and undisciplined. I imagined standing, projecting the light point generated, visualizing it was shooting out from my chest center into the world. My invisible ink.

As I stood and engaged, person by person, situation to situation, plan to plan, or dream to dream, I found myself activating my superhero laser. All concentrated into a light beam reaching out, influencing, as well as beaconing to other light sources near and far. The new metaphor began relating to life as a spiritual sport; dense and intense, but it all makes sense.

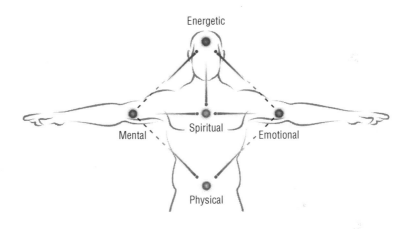

Alchemy and Manifesting

The idea that consciousness is merely a secretion or manifestation of a complex net of electrical impulses working within the mass of cells in our brain, has been discredited; however, there remains the problem of consciousness and its relationship to material form—the mind/brain problem.

It is difficult to hold focus on a singular point for long stretches of time. Our brain is ever moving, jumping from one perception, feeling, thought, to another. Concentration is good in spurts. Like the quantum nature of matter, the more we try to hold our consciousness to a fixed point, the greater the uncertainty in its energy becomes until it hits a certain energetic point. This is a tipping point between rebellion and submission. The storm before the calm. Work through the uncertainty.

When we focus and narrow our consciousness to a fixed center, mind is likely to suddenly jump with a great rush of energy to some seemingly unrelated aspect from threads of stimuli. In some ways, the relational database doesn't want to be told not to do its job.

We all have such experiences each moment of the day. We try to focus our mind upon some problem only to suddenly experience a shift to some other domain in ourselves, another image or emotional current intruding, then vanishing like a virtual particle in quantum theory. Fleeting thoughts they are called. Distractions that disable.

We should no longer relate to our brain as vast circuitry powering our perception of time and space. If we trace a nerve impulse down to its root, there lies a quantum uncertainty within a sea of probability. The sea of probability becomes a sea of potentiality. Like a cello concerto, an opera that opens the heart, disparate entities come together in beauty, rhythm, and flow.

When our consciousness focuses to a point, and we concentrate on some abstract problem or outer phenomenon, the physical events in our brain, the pattern of impulses, shifts in some ordered way. In a sense, the probability waves of many quantum systems in different parts of the brain are brought into resonance, and consciousness is momentarily able to create a positive pattern that manifests physically. The thought, feeling, perception is momentarily earthed in physical reality, brought from the realm of the spiritually potential into outer actuality.

This focused ordering of the probability waves of many quantum systems requires an enormous amount of energy, but this can be borrowed in the quantum sense for a short instant of time. Thus, we have through this quantum borrowing a virtual quantum state which is the physical embodiment of a thought, feeling, etc.

However, as this can only be held for a short time, the quantum debt must be paid and the point of our awareness jumps to some other quantum state, perhaps in another region of the brain. Thus, our thoughts are jumbled up with emotions, perceptions, fantasy, and images.

Although our point of consciousness lives at this enormously fast speed, our brain which transforms this into a pattern of electrochemical activity runs at a much slower rate. Between creating each pattern, our spark of consciousness must wait almost an eternity for this to be manifested on the physical level. Perhaps this may account for the sense we all have sometimes of taking an enormous leap in consciousness or traveling through vast realms of ideas, or flashes of images, in what is only a fleeting moment.

Everything is Connected

In quantum mechanics, it is referred to as 'entanglement,' the field of pure potentiality. As with everything in life, because of its energetic construct, and regardless of the perceived space that exists between particles or how we see matter, everything is connected.

For every action, there is a reaction. In acknowledging light, we must acknowledge there is dark. For each quark, there is an antiquark. For all that we can do, there are things we think or feel we cannot do, will or will not do, have or can't have. For all positive statements, there are negating ones; for every glass that is half full, there are containers which are half empty. In a circumference of 360°, there is a halfway point at 180°.

For each perspective, there is an opposing viewpoint. We all have programming to support right, virtuous, and moral, or we have intentions from a less evolved source introducing 'wrong,' malice, or immoral. Such is the nature of our existence. In the aspects of duality, there is co-location. It is us in our humanity whereby we choose which space we occupy.

Coming full circle, we all travel paths encompassing common themes, to a playground where choices are constantly manufactured. Whether we analyze the atomic, energetic, kinetic, or frenetic, we will be given enough proof that all elements, in some way, are connected.

In the inherent duality of existence, we must appreciate not only the importance of choice but the freedom of perspective on how we choose. Our perspectives obviously influence how we act, what we think, and how we are triggered emotionally. The mental realm is where we can exert much control over our emotional health.

A positive perspective keeps our machine and programming vitalized and functioning with great efficiency. Because the mental realm is our source of thought form, harnessing the mind to maximize our output is crucial to not only success but happiness as well. This is the perspective in the cliché of 'everything has a silver lining.' Remember, how emotional disturbances affect us on a cellular level, influences the matter of every being within range of its frequency. In duality, we begin to comprehend all possibilities because all possibilities are encompassed. Fully embracing this implication is of the highest magnitude should we desire to change behavior, communities, and lives.

There are many occurrences in our physical body that we define as nothing short of miraculous: the functioning of organs, tissue regeneration, the electrical impulses that keep our heart beating, consciousness, electronic messaging and delivery, etc. If we go from the outside in, we know what it is like to touch our skin, feel or see blood, feel anxious or nervous, be joyful, understand objects viscerally by texture, color, shape.

We don't question our internal structure is all-knowing. We do in fact trust this process. Most of us don't go around every day chanting the mantra: *May my blood keep pumping; May my blood keep pumping* . . . It is what it is, and we just deal with the Yield of all the invisible, semi-invisible processes at work. We wake up functioning every day, not interfering, just harvesting and harnessing.

The nature of our world is a tale of opposites, in absolutely everything that exists. The composite of the Tao reminds us how not only opposites coexist, but that opposites are part and parcel to balance in systems. The forces and elements contained in duality highlight that either side, either entity, can be chosen. A second grader once put forth the proverbial conundrum for a young mind, the 'why do bad things happen' question. Because people choose to make bad things happen, my dear.

As such, it becomes necessary to delve deeply into the mechanism of choice, how there exist energetic threads that attach way beyond our individual choice to many things in the world. Why do things happen in the world? Primarily because people choose to make things happen. If spiritual proverbs preach non-judgment, who decides, let alone define, what is proper or improper condemnation?

There are endless examples in endless categories of life about things apparently unrelated, that are indeed, very related. As human forms on a spherical planet that has thousands of variations of lifeform, processes, developments, simultaneous reactions, how can we not truly believe that indeed everything is connected? Things have changed over a billion years, but aspects of connectivity have not.

Clichés, while trite, are very profound concepts, which when pondered and experienced, are expansionary to consciousness. Take a moment to remember those situations where you mutter the words, 'wow, what a coincidence I ran into you.' Was it really a coincidence or was it convergence? Maybe that coincidence is simply God's way of making sure you are paying attention. Fated, or just on your way to meet Fate?

Again, the examples could be limitless, but in fact can very often be much, much more than just a banana being a banana. Remember in life as a metaphor, when you peel that banana, toss the skin towards a trash bin, miss, the peel is on the ground. Someone may ultimately slip on that peel, fall, and then they have to confront the absurdity of a banana being more than just a banana. If they discover you threw the banana peel, there is a personal injury attorney a phone call away.

In their reality, that banana may have just assisted them to skin their hand or knee, or worse, crack a tailbone from a fall. You just never know how absurd life can be, but also in the absurdity what it may be trying to show you. Stay open to all the possibilities.

Remember, energetically, everything is connected.

Heart-Sparking Performance

The most dramatic of our physical components, the heart represents the 'magic' of life and living—a muscle, like any muscle, that can be developed, trained, hurt or cracked. For the most part, it is one make, one model. Of course, there are minute differences across humanity. One may be relatively strong; one may be burdened with a bad part. Sometimes it stops when it decides. Sometimes it is broken by another. However, living from our hearts is where true strength and balance are discovered.

Love is responsible for 'moving mountains.' Its force can shift us, creating a prism with the combined light of our desires. This is why breath meditation teaches to ascertain the heart rhythms across the range of the breath cycle. There is a taking in, and a letting go. In time, a drop into the subtler layers. There is something magical that happens when we can focus this light beam into the world. The intensity and capability honed from stabilizing and balancing five contributing circles of consciousness. One flip of the switch and the laser beam of light hums to life.

No doubt there are moments in our days when our heart is heavy, or light, maybe troubled, possibly triumphant. It is barraged with demands while it supports many things happening. In two dimensions, a mass of muscle and memory; in three dimensions, a metaphor for creation.

The equal sign in the equation: life = spiritual sport. In three dimensional aspects, it is the transformer which sends our light point into the world, our laser beam, our invisible ink. If we approach life as a spiritual sport, this is where we learn by experience and want to become something distinctly powerful. When we perform, we also transform.

The theme has a slight variation depending on translations, yet it bases down to the same message. Whether in Persian, Grecian, Buddhist, Chinese, Egyptian, Christian, Mohammedan, Hindu, Roman, Hebrew, Sufi, Islamic, is expressed the same wish for man's behavior toward man. Preached through all spiritual cultures and texts, all grandmothers' laps, is this same premise.

Treat others as you yourself would want to be treated. Why would you ever wish something on someone that you would never want to happen to you and those you love?

In today's increasingly fundamental and secular age of religious camps, cultures of violence, areas of oppression, the pressure is on, the distortion is greater. There is so much more pressure to carve out our fiefdom of sanity, regardless of the consequences. Maybe it is done in a neighborhood with vigilantes, maybe it is done in a country by deciding to war, maybe it is done by a community deciding a certain group doesn't have the same rights.

We have a chicken and egg dilemma occurring. How can we treat our brothers the way we want to be treated, yet not fear our hearts will be trampled in the act? How does one stay open in the face of grand challenges? Can you really be a Zen master, coffee in one hand, device in the other, riding a skateboard merrily across your dashboard without spilling or dropping your phone?

This message we know and hear is one of love; the hugely missing component is tolerance. It is only through the power of love where understanding tolerance is discovered. Why? Because it is tough to have your toes stepped on, and then in reaction not want to bonk that person on the head, gettin' all righteous. We need, and want to protect 'our territory.'

The paradox is acute because as we all want to manifest, all want something. Tolerance stands alongside forgiveness as some of the hardest spiritual refinements one will experience. It concerns beliefs, attitudes, and the dark side of knowledge, namely ignorance. When a loved one does something that sets us off, it is possible to shift, better serving the situation with patience and detached observation, two traits found deeply ingrained in the heart-center.

Individually there will come a time when you must travel inward, beckoning truth from the heart-center. At the root of it all, it is the only place that will ultimately reveal, in real-time, what is for the best and highest good of all who share earth's playing fields. Learning to differentiate intuition vs. head trips may take you some time, but in short order, like distinguishing good proteins from the bad fats, is obvious.

At this point, you can expect to find the expression of what happens when we channel energies from our four circles of consciousness through the heart. In this alchemy, we all have, and find something different, has been created. Consider your invisible ink. The processes we will use to paint our pictures, write our compositions, lead others, manifesting change in ourselves, out into the world. It is invisible only until revealed by another. It can end in the discovery of your divine, or it will serve as your sacred starting point.

Don't overthink it.

Heart spark it!

JRx

Everything comes to a point, literally and figuratively. It's a group of concepts when applied in consistent practice produce tangible experiences. Four realms, four circles of consciousness, mental, emotional, physical and energetic, broken down, cleaned, inspected, lubricated and rebuilt. Knowledge accumulated is power. With knowledge, and now experience, we construct a solid game plan for whatever we need to accomplish.

Base principles embedded in each realm are now connected and integrated. A vision, thoughtform, an idea sealed in a positive perspective raises emotional intelligence. Our 'vision quest' blends and concentrates the best energies of mental/ emotional, balancing the push/pull, our giving and receiving. We are reminded to see things differently, shift what we can control, become creative versus being consumed, reactive.

Knowing our physical system must perform optimally for any push to the top, attention is dedicated to understanding more about what we consume. There is respect for the challenge. Pain will be encountered, but what kind of pain is it? Balancing our energetic grid, we employ metaphysical fuels that help us cross the finish line.

Evaluating the integrity of our attachments, we can leverage duality, providing a profound perspective shift as we practice detachment via sacred separation. Giving up something we love, energetically releasing things, objects, people, untenable situations, we come back with a new connection. A fresh connection sharpens clarity around what is for our best and highest good.

From these four points, comes another. Truths in each realm converge in our heart-center, magnifying in amplitude. Leveraging the creative force embedded, channeling all positive energies into convergence, we are by definition, preparing to receive an epiphany.

JRxercise

Combining many elements of this path work, a fundamental manifestation exercise helps us to find some proof in the power of heart-sparking. Affirmations 201. Via a process taking us to a point where we can crystallize our asks, the task is to create a simple wish list for things you want to happen. Whether agnostic or already a preacher, don't fret. This isn't a God conversation. This is harnessing what we can control.

AFFIRMATIONS

There are a few ground rules when doing written affirmations. So as not to bleed the issue to unconsciousness, I will say keep winning the lottery or healing someone of their cancer off the list. The idea is to create, whereby we find reflected back to us, its appearance in everyday living, in a short window of time. Your list can be up to ten items, but generally, seven to eight good constructs are ample. For every two personal asks created, one affirmation needs to be created for someone else. So, in a list of seven, four are focus on yourself, and three are set as intentions for others.

Over time doing affirmations, we get better crafting our asks in writing. It always harked back a principle a past teacher used to say with a wry smile. His words of 'it takes nine years to learn how to pray' is a lengthy campfire talk, but the overriding message was spirit doesn't discriminate energy. We learn we must be mindful of what we ask for in life.

Start using two sheets of paper. One to scribble and scratch through, then another that will be your clean copy. Now the thought process begins. What on earth do I want to manifest in the next couple of weeks let's say? As you go about your routine, shopping, conversing, networking, dining, browsing, begin with some tangible object requests. Samples:

Let's say you need a new outfit for an important corporate function or social event. Try seeing how precise you could be listing what the outfit would like for you. Of course, it would be better on sale, so list that as well. Color, texture, design, how great it would make you feel, how it would go with x, y, or z accessories. See it, feel it, touch it, smell the new smell, all with a smile on your face and a happy vibe in your heart. Maybe you want to find a new Martini shaker, funky glasses, or even that perfect car you still haven't found at your price yet. Visualize away.

For the affirmations where you want to focus on others there are many ways these asks can go, but again let's start and stay with the more straightforward. One is an affirmation I have found myself employing over time when friends or loved ones are dealing with a health challenge. The American Cancer Society support group I utilized is responsible for the current philosophical approach I use as someone changed my whole perspective on helping others in the ways we can.

While I was confronting my own cancer diagnosis, someone in support shared a perspective that has stayed with me. Boiled down, they said you can continue to pray for a miracle, miracle cure, but make sure in your prayers you demand they have one, really strong feeling day amid bad ones. So now I do. Now my affirmation reads something like the following: I want to hear, see, Jane/John have a magical day, laughing, happy, strong one day out of the next three.

Putting intentions around (emotional) relief, asking for someone else to experience an epiphany for their best and highest good. Maybe you get creative and combine affirmations. You ask for something to manifest in your daily world that isn't a financial burden for you but would be a great gift to give, or something you can then give to someone else knowing it would brighten their day.

Bless a one-dollar bill with all the best wishes you can muster, instruct that it be used for something spiritually productive, then give it away.

Co-create the coincidence to appear. Review your list, reviewing fully present, feeling the hope, wants and desires that are heart sourced.

- Within seven days the perfect outfit will present itself. It's unique, it's different, it's only in my size and it's on sale. (Vision quest in detail, see you smile, see yourself in the mirror, etc., etc.)

- Something unique for my son or daughter's birthday. What he/she would have fun discovering, and that would advance their happiness quotient. (Vision quest the compartments if you can't specify exactly. An electronic device, outdoor gear, self-improvement, camp, challenge or concert). Present something that is in the budget and that will put smiles on all.

- I manifest to come across 'X' kind of shoes, boots, footwear for this outfit. Literally walking into a place, on sale.

- I create discovering the perfect piece of furniture for that space John and I are struggling to design. Something that is bold, pulls the whole energy of our project together perfectly, shape, color, grain, wood, style, price. Where energy is balanced, feng shui proper.

- In the next 72 hours, I pray for Jane, that she experiences visible relief from her discomfort. Laughing, smiling, in good spirits, unexplainable. Free her for one day from her suffering.

- Networking I am going to run into some new people that will create a mutually beneficial (financial) relationship for both groups. Friends of friends, at the right place at exactly the right time, my vibration attracts what is for the best and highest good leading me, and my team, to success.

Fine-tune your list that has no more fixes or adjustments after rereading and deeply pondering the vision for each. Ideally, in green or red ink, transfer your final points onto a clean sheet of paper (keep mistakes as minimal as possible). Once you have a final written list, find a sacred safe zone, fold in half, seal with your imaginary power and mojo, and set away for twenty-four hours.

Day 2, retrieve your list. You are preparing to read through one more time, full energy being injected into your commands. Take the list after review, place over your heart. Smiling, heart open, ask spirit to reflect back the energies to manifest. After review, burn the list (bathroom or outside-you can hold over the toilet until it gets down to a comfortable corner then toss into water). As it burns, repeat out loud "So shall it be!"

In time and with practice, you will have fun seeing coincidences you co-created. Applications, clarity of asks become more advanced, refined as we rise through a few epiphanies that come our way.

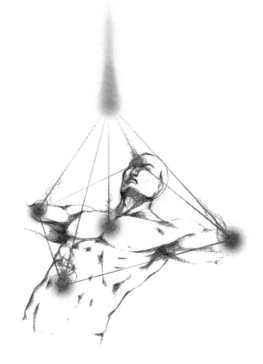

POSTSCRIPT

Social Consciousness and Time

Every so often as a young adult in sports, you would get the 'there is no 'I' in team' speech. Grammatically obvious, but far from operational truth. In every team dynamic or collective with a mission statement, a grounded sense of self is highly valued. There is a positive benefit to limiting unpredictability while moving towards a goal. Grounded generally reflects elevated emotional intelligence which implies stability.

While the focus of this book centered on the individual accumulating more knowledge along a path towards mastery, it is important to acknowledge the duality of individual and society. Dual realities, if you will, often with clashing principles.

From a timing standpoint, the release of this book touches on a societal wave of backlash and reaction stemming from a density of pressure points. Consciousness is putting up a mirror forcing us to rethink conservation, creative cultivation of ecosystems and natural resources.

Instead, what seems to dominate a societal phase is more reactive. All that is embodied is a lack of grounding principles mirrored as a new state of being in America. I am not for or against any one particular executive order that so far has flown off the White House desk. Nor am I protesting global leadership decisions, another race for nuclear capability. I am holding space for unpredictability and impulsiveness to one day find diplomacy and restraint.

I, too, find myself holding my breath, catching my mind drift off into places mostly reactive, creating unnecessary mental chatter. The obvious is I am not alone. Quickly, culturally we are dividing into two camps, supporting or boycotting. It has become cooler to express, but equally cool to bash. It's always been this way, some will say. Maybe, maybe not.

Echoing sentiments put forth by a fellow Stanford athlete alumnus, Senator Cory Booker (NJ), it is time for our individual performance to reflect how we maintain a creative energetic response to challenges we encounter in society. As difficult as it may be, balance the mental and emotional, meeting at the center point of heart, striving to create harmony in the face of bias.

Factions are fracturing off like Antarctic glaciers in a warming climate. Nationalism, big business, and bullying by the pen and fabricated media are the new policy normal. Temperaments are rising along with temperatures creating an emotional hothouse effect. *I can't believe* . . . the new negative normal. These are times to heed the power necessary to change. When we truly dwell in the heart of all matters, hopefully, a compassionate shift will occur as we progress and continue to plunder. From plastics in our ocean to plastic explosives killing people.

Somehow, someway, knowing we are more capable than what we are demonstrating must hark to the inherent integrity of voice into right action and good intentions. In some ways, now is the time to re-establish our roots, reflecting back to the objectives upon which our country was formed, fairness, right action, civic responsibility, commerce, and service. Help a brother or sister out.

We read and digest weekly how Mother Earth as an operating system is experiencing change. Her coolant, oil, remains the commodity of choice. As the drain continues, consumption continues to burn. There are shifts in climate patterns, but does this absolutely mean there is drastic climate change? As within so without. Everything is connected.

Strive to maintain a balance between the dualistic containers we universally deal with. Imagine with love, constantly injecting spiritual intentions that everything will be for the best and highest good for us as one nation under God. For Mother Earth, for ourselves, for our children, our communities and circles. Balance a negative reaction with a positive intention or creation, material or metaphysical. Blend your IQ and EQ, shifting what you can control, then perform because your heart has sparked.

As a society, we are lacking accountability for what isn't happening. There are pressing matters to tend to, so it is about time. I would very much enjoy my daughter growing up in a world where right action is a powerful motivator to young shapers. Like Bhutan, a happiness index of sorts.

There is much more at stake than allowing ourselves to perpetuate a fairy tale dominated by princesses and Peter Pans. Good performances take detailed preparation. Change involves desire, endurance, and courage. With all the diligence you can muster, revisit your toolbox.

All paths lead to something. There are times when you follow a path to its literal end, a finish line equating completion. But sometimes the path takes you somewhere, and it's not where you thought it would be. You thought you were finished, but not so much. The path has led you to a launch point, a base camp. From there, you still have more to do. That path had a specific purpose.

To create new files of information it is important to put concepts into application. Following the 'we all want proof' adage, doubters must find their kernels of personal truth, conviction. Thus, to expand from concept to conviction, employ the five-step pep talk. It will produce glimpses of power in what you plan to create because you are dynamic as an alchemist. Creating an experience gives us a reference point allowing us to define our personal truth, consciously. You can't say you understand or know something until you have the experience to relate. Now, let's get it done, as a circle, for all circles.

Stop.
Snap.
Shift.
Success.
Satisfied.

ABOUT THE AUTHOR

Jon's evolved relationship to performance and change emerges in his perspective encouraging a more conscious connection to all that we undertake and co-create. *Life, The Spiritual Sport*, is a relationship metaphor which emphasizes blending all things physical with all things metaphysical to create, and relate, from the heart. Weaving decades of personal experience, spiritual teachings, successes and failures, themes of 'conscious creation,' 'sacred separation,' 'intentional force' help to inspire and motivate meaningful change and action, 'in your circle, for all circles.'

Marticulating from Stanford with dual degrees, he is a volleyball Hall of Fame inductee. Upon graduation, he bypassed the Wall Street investment banking craze to make the best of an opportunity to represent the US at the Olympics. The US national men's volleyball team, after winning gold in Los Angeles in 1984, went on to post a remarkable 197-31 record over a four-year period, winning the sport's triple crown in the process (consecutive champions, 1985 World Cup, 1986 World Championships, 1988 Olympic Games.

A native of West Los Angeles, Jon is a writer, producer with a number of published works. He is still teaching, preaching and screeching his truths and tenets as a U18 club volleyball coach for boys and girls in the Bay Area. Jon's daughter, Ayden, is a standout club volleyball player who lives and trains in Southern California. Activities and loves include all things nature, animals, the mystical and the magical.